Jan. 8, 1987

Michael, I hope
this book will help!,
Best Regards,
Charles A. Peterson

ISBN No. 0-9614806-0-2

How You Can Leave The City
FOREVER!

SECRETS OF EARNING A LIVING IN THE COUNTRY

Charles A. Peterson

Library of Congress Catalog Card Number: 85-90354

Cover illustration by Terri Lennon

Copyright © 1985, by Charles A. Peterson, Peterson Publications, Ltd.
All Rights Reserved
Printed in The United States of America
B & B Printers, Gunnison, INC., Gunnison, Colorado 81230

ISBN No. 0-9614806-0-2

PREFACE

YOU NEED THIS BOOK IF:

...You have dreamed of leaving your life in the city, and moving to the country – but weren't sure how to make the move. This book will not only give you all the information you need to make this move, but will explain why you should do it as soon as possible.

...You feel trapped by a job that grinds you down and leaves you with a feeling of frustration.

...Your worry about the education your children are receiving, both in and out of the classroom.

...You fear for the safety of your family as they do simple things such as shopping, going to the movies, walking to school.

...You are tired of spending a major portion of your life commuting back and forth to a job you don't really enjoy, often leaving before the sun is up and returning when it's pitch dark.

...You have this uneasy feeling that something is wrong with the life you are living now, but you can't put your finger on it. As you look at the mass of humanity around you, you worry about inflation, crime, nuclear war, and a decline in the moral and spiritual values you were raised with.

...You sense that your job with the "Acme Corporation" may not be a secure as your boss would like you to believe.

...You have difficulty remembering the last time you went fishing, took your family on a picnic, or just took a quiet walk and DIDN'T worry about being mugged, offended by all the trash laying around, or sharing your quiet spot with someone whose idea of enjoying nature was a radio turned up past "loud" so that everyone within a quarter of a mile could hear the latest noise that passes for music.

If you identify with any of these scenarios, then you need this book. Turn the pages of this book and you will learn how you can make your move to the country, how to find a job, what you can expect, and more importantly, why you should make the move within the next twelve months.

TABLE OF CONTENTS

Preface

Introduction i

Chapter 1 1
    Why Living in a Small Town May be Essential
    To Your Health and Wealth In The Future.

Chapter 2 7
    What Does The Future Hold?

Chapter 3 27
    Preparing For The Move

Chapter 4 39
    Earning A Living In The Country

Chapter 5 47
    Successful Country Businesses
    — 25 Examples —

Chapter 6 105
    Summing It All Up

Recommended Reading List 109

Newsletters 112

Free Pamphlets 114

INTRODUCTION

As you drove or rode to work this morning, did you marvel at the attractive scenery? Did you enjoy the beauty of the country side as you and your commuting companions drove to work among cars filled with other friendly commuters? If your radio was on, did you hear about all of the good things that are happening in your community, or did the news fill you in on all the crimes of violence that had occurred the night before? When you arrived fresh at your job, did you approach your appointed task with a feeling of excitement and expectation, or did you have the feeling that no one except your immediate supervisor would even notice if you didn't show up? Do you worry if your wife and children are home alone?

If you are fed up with your current lifestyle, if you have had it with smog, commuting, crime, fear, rudeness, and the city life in general, then maybe it's time you looked into changing your life style. I had many of the same feelings and longings that you have now, and just as you can, I made a move to the country.

I live in a small town. It was chosen with a great deal of thought and preparation. My wife and children moved here from a large metropolitan area because we wanted our children to grow up in a rural environment. I am certain that many of you that are reading this book would like to do the same thing, and I intend to give you all the necessary information to move you off dead center, and proceed with YOUR move to the country.

I see ominous storm clouds on the horizon. As I write this, the stated budget deficit exceeds 200 billion dollars. The stock market set an all time volume record yesterday because the economy "slowed down". Figure that one out! Crimes of violence continue to increase in metropolitan areas, and life in the cities is becoming more and more of a struggle. There is a definite feeling of gloom and doom among thinking people all over the country -- a feeling that something is about to happen, and that events are beyond their ability to control them. But let me tell you a story, the final straw that caused us to leave the city and the rat race.

We had just purchased an older home in an older area of the city where we lived. We had chosen this area on purpose. There were lots of stately trees, the neighborhood was well cared for and the school system was fully integrated. This was important to us, because we wanted our children to grow up around other children of different races. More important to me, I wanted the school to be integrated *economically* as well as racially. The neighborhood we chose was perfect in this regard. Then disaster struck. A Federal Judge, in his wisdom, decided that it made no difference that our school had fulfilled all its integration requirements, the children from our little school had to be bussed across town to achieve "racial balance". Our appeals to logic fell on deaf ears, and I learned one of my first lessons about bureaucrats -- they don't respond to logic, only to pain.

My wife and I sat down and gave the matter a lot of thought. We looked at the current problems that we were having with the school, smog, crime, rudeness and a decline in the general quality of life. We decided that the answer for us was to move to a small rural community where we would know our neighbors by name, and the schools would be totally integrated -- because there would only be one school! We have never regretted our decision.

The prophet Isaiah warned, "Woe unto them that join house to house, that lay field to field, till there be no place, that they may be placed alone in the midst of the earth". Now please don't accuse me of misinterpreting Isaiah. City life certainly has its place -- but by the same token, life in the country has blessings that you can't imagine until you've lived there.

You may be twenty years old, and tired of the problems of the city. You may be a senior citizen who just wants to find a place where you can retire in peace and dignity. What ever your current age or lifestyle, if you have ever dreamed of moving to a quiet rural area, this book is written for *you*.

It is my hope that this book will give you the incentive you need to make YOUR move to the country.

Charles A. Peterson
Gunnison, Colorado
August 3, 1984

Chapter 1

Why Living in a Small Town May Be Essential To Your Health and Wealth In The Future.

One of the greatest advantages of living in a small community is what I refer to as the "People Factor", and, as we race toward the future, this factor will become more and more important. As I write this chapter, I am reminded that my neighbor is in the hospital, and the happiness that I felt for him and his family when his son told me that the anticipated operation was not going to be necessary. I am also reminded of my elderly neighbor who lost his wife last month, and how his neighbors, family, and friends came to share his grief and to console him. When I lived in the City, I didn't know the people that lived across the street from me, let alone two blocks away. Now this condition could have been corrected--I could have introduced myself and my family to my City neighbors, but that simply wasn't the way things were done. At the present time, I know virtually 75% of the residents of my community by their first names. These people, in turn, know me, my wife and my three children. They know what kind of people we are -- our strong points, and our weaknesses --just as we know theirs. Whatever the future holds, I am secure in the knowledge that we are surrounded by people that we know and trust, and that we have nothing to fear from our neighbors. As the future unfolds, this freedom from fear will be one of the greatest advantages of rural living.

Each evening as I read our States' largest newspaper, I am overwhelmed by the crimes that are reported, almost on a daily basis -- murder, rape, child molestation and abuse, children that have simply disappeared, pornography, the elderly reduced to eating dog food, police in the schools to prevent racial battles, and smog alerts. As a parent, I am shocked beyond belief that day care centers in California and New York have been fronts for child pornographers and sexual deviates. My heart goes out to these parents, but I can't help but think that these terrible crimes could have been avoided if the parents of these children had been neighbors of the people that ran the day care centers. They would have been able to sense that something was amiss.

Now don't get me wrong. I am well aware that some of these things go on in small towns as well, but the odds of them happening to you or your family are greatly reduced, simply because of the small size of the town. Which brings me to one of my pet theories (I refer to it as *Peterson's Population Postulate*). I believe that 1% of the population is crazy, deviate, loony, cuckoo — this means New York City, with its population of 12 million, has 120,000 or more crazies running around. In my little town of 5,000, you have 50, but here is the important part: YOU KNOW WHO THEY ARE!

As inflation increases across our great land (which it will), and as the bureaucrats try to control inflation by attempting to break economic law through wage and price controls (as they most surely will), one of the safest and healthiest places to live will be in rural America. When inflation and envy begin to destroy wealth in the cities, as the "have nots" blame the "haves" for their predicament, doesn't it make a great deal of sense to live in an area that still looks upon crime as wrong -- that still respects the traditional values of hard work, love of family, Churches and a belief in God? An area that has a respect for moral values, property and a basic honesty? Doesn't it make sense to send your children to a school that still believes in teaching a student to read and write, and not base progress on the teaching of some exotic social program? Wouldn't you prefer that your children attend a school where they are not fearful of being mugged, or worse yet, attacked because of their race or physical appearance?

Later in this book as we discuss inflation, what causes it, and where it will ultimately lead, it will become more obvious why living in a rural area is essential to your family's health and well-being. For the moment, I would just point out to you that many small towns are in physically beautiful locations, with many advantages that simply aren't available in the cities, such as skiing, hunting, fishing, boating, hiking and so forth. Another real advantage is that the cost of living is usually lower in small rural towns.

It is going to be more difficult to physically make the move to the country as time progresses. As inflation increases in the future, it will be harder and harder for you to "cash out" of you home equity in the city, and purchase property in the country because the pool of available mortgage funds will dry up. As the fixed rate mortgage becomes more and more a thing of the past, it will become increasingly difficult to sell your property without resorting to "owner financing", or some other exotic form of financing to make the sale. Doesn't it make sense to start planning now -- <u>today</u> to make the move that will be necessary to protect your family and your assets?

As you continue in this book, it will be apparent to you that I really enjoy the country life. In an attempt to be fair, I should point out that there are some disadvantages to rural living. The biggest drawback that I have found is the limited economic base of a small town. Many businesses or professions simply won't be able to make it because there just aren't enough customers or clients to support them. Yet there always seems to be room for a good new competitor with a strong capital base. If you are bent on being a millionaire, it is more difficult to accomplish in the country than it is in the city, simply because the economic base is smaller.

When I make occasional visits to the city, I am always impressed by the sheer volume of people driving up and down the freeways. I keep thinking that if each of these people has $10.00 in their pocket, the amount of wealth driving on these freeways must be incredible. If you can figure a way to capture just a portion of this money, you could become a wealthy person. It is easier for an entrepreneur to make money in the city, simply because there is a larger population base with which to work.

Later in this book, I will give you details about businesses and professions that are successful in small towns now, businesses that I have researched and KNOW have been successful for their owners. If you are creative and aggressive, you will be able to find your place in the country, but it makes sense that the limited size of a rural community would make it more difficult for a brain surgeon to make a living than it would for a general practitioner.

Another drawback to a small town can be a lack of cultural advantages. This may or may not be a big concern to you, but one way to assure yourself of not moving to a cultural desert is to pick a town that has a small college. By choosing a town that has a small college, you assure yourself of being able to attend plays, band concerts, film festivals, recitals and guest lecturers. The college will give the town a tone that a non-college town just doesn't have. The students make up a segment of the population that make good employees, and have an unbelievable amount of disposable income. My experience has been that 98.5% of the student body are really great people. They are fun-loving, honest and good citizens. I am sure that there are exceptions to "my" college, but my experience has been good. This may be because the college in the town where I live appeals to students that are trying to get away from some of the same things that I moved from the city to get away from.

You will have to make the decision about how important cultural events are in the town that you choose, but you must be truthful with yourself -- how many cultural events do you attend now? The fact that you live in a rural area does not stop you from taking your family to the city for a weekend, and visiting the museums, zoos, theaters and shopping centers. In fact, these trips can be a very important part of your family's education and recreation. I find that some people visit more of these places and events *after* they moved to the country than they did when they lived in the city.

Technology in the form of satellite receiving dishes has enabled television signals to be received virtually any place in the United States. Whether you want to view opera, sports events, old movies or reruns, these dishes enable you to watch television 24 hours a day if you so desire. The small town that I live in has cable television, four FM stereo radio stations, and one AM station. Wherever you choose to live, you will be able to keep informed, entertained and educated by the proper use of technology that is available today. I should also point out that some of the time you now spend watching television and attending cultural events will be taken up by fishing, hunting, boating, hiking, photography, skiing, snowmobiling and taking your family on picnics. After all, isn't that part of the reason you want to move to the country?

Another purported disadvantage to small town living is what I refer to as "the small town hierarchy". These communities do have their pecking orders, but this can be an advantage as well as a disadvantage. Most of the businesses and banks in a small town have been owned by the same families for many years. They have seen a lot of strangers come and go, and many of them have adopted a "wait and see' attitude toward newcomers. The reason for this attitude is because they have been "taken" before by people that have moved in from the city, and they are being cautious. Once you have established yourself as an honorable individual or family, they tend to go out of their way to help you. In the eleven years that I've lived in my small town, I've had bankers make me loans that *I* wouldn't have made to me when I worked as a banker.

Gossip is prevalent everywhere, but some would tell you that it is more prevalent in a small community. I have come to believe that a lot of what would normally pass for gossip is actually concern for the individual involved. In a small community people care for each other and are concerned. If a family is having financial or marital difficulties, their neighbors are concerned and want to help if possible. I find this attitude far superior to the "You leave me alone, and I'll leave you alone" attitude in the cities. As one of my friends said to me, if you are going to "Mess Around", a small town probably isn't the best place to do it.

I'm sure that I've missed a disadvantage or two, but I must point out that the disadvantages of small town life are so far outweighed by the advantages that there simply is no comparison.

Chapter 2

What Does The Future Hold?

Will it be Inflation? Probably more rubbish has been written and spoken about the "causes" of inflation than on any other single subject. I am constantly amazed when our national leaders discuss inflation, because it becomes apparent that they don't know what inflation is either. The other conclusion is that they know, but are afraid to tell the American people. It is more convenient to place the blame for inflation on the "bad boy" of the moment, whether it is the Arab oil producers, labor unions, Big Business with their "obscene" profits (I've always wondered at what point profits cease being obscene and become chaste), or unpatriotic people who are selling out their country by purchasing those "non-producing" metals, silver and gold. The fact is that none of these things are the *cause* of inflation, but are all the *result* of inflation.

Webster's Third New International Dictionary defines inflation as follows: *"in-fla-tion: an increase in the volume of money and credit relative to available goods resulting in a substantial and continuing rise in the general price level."* You will notice that no mention is made of the Arabs, labor unions, big business or the buying or selling of gold or silver. Now who controls *"the volume of money and credit"*? Do any of these "bad boys" have any control over *"the volume of money and credit"*? Of course not. Only our friendly, benevolent government has that control. Is it possible that we have a President and Vice President, House and Senate, Cabinet, Supreme Court and bureaucracy that do not possess a Webster's Third New International Dictionary? Do you think it would help things if I sent them mine?

When I was in college, I was fortunate (blessed) to have an excellent Economics Professor. He made the "dismal science" of economics come alive, and cut through all of the gibberish to expose the fundamental laws that govern this body of knowledge. He died shortly after my first semester, but the short period of time that I studied under him as a young man left an indelible impression on me. When I started my business career I kept feeling that something was wrong with the definitions of inflation, money, interest, gold, silver and so forth that I was hearing from the politicians and reading about in the papers. By some quirk of fate, probably while I was frequenting used book stores, I came across a copy of "Economics in One Lesson" by Henry Hazlitt. This one book seemed to confirm what my old Economics Professor was saying, and gave me an incentive to study the works of Ludwig von Mises, Murray Rothbard, Gary North, Adam Smith and F.A. Hayek. Quite frankly, these guys scared the hell out of me, but I guess the truth is always frightening when you have been told lies by those you want to trust.

If you are interested in learning more about economics, please check the reading list at the back of this book. I'll promise you that you will never be the same if you will study any of these authors. If your experience with economics has been bad (I'm convinced that every Ph.D. candidate for a degree in economics *must* take at least one

Chapter 2

course in "how to confuse your students with big, hard to pronounce words," and "how to be boring"), I'll promise you that your opinion will be completely changed if you'll read Henry Hazlitt's book.

One of the nice things you find out when you study the books I've mentioned above is that economic laws are just as reliable as physical laws. Just as the law of gravity affects a baseball thrown into the air, it also affects a cannon ball that is fired into the air. *If a physical law works on a small scale, then it will also work on a large scale.* It makes no difference whether you throw a baseball, a cannon ball, or a space vehicle into the air, they will continue to move in the direction of the thrust force until gravity slows their speed and they fall to earth (or in the case of a space vehicle, achieve orbit).

In economics, Gresham's Law *(gresh-am's law: an observation in economics; when two coins are equal in debt-paying value but unequal in intrinsic value, the one having the lesser intrinsic value tends to remain in circulation and the other to be hoarded or exported as bullion)* affects the United States, just as it did ancient Rome. Gresham's Law is simplified as follows: Bad money drives out good money. One of my greatest economic memories is President Lyndon Baines Johnson stating on television in 1964 that anyone who was saving pre-1964 dimes, quarters and half-dollars was a fool. He stated that the United States government had enough silver stockpiled to keep the price of silver at $1.29 forever. A small, simply law, Gresham's Law, but as you check your pockets for pre-1964 dimes, quarters and half-dollars, you decide which was stronger, Gresham's Law or the President and the United States Government.

Just an aside, but another example of Gresham's Law is at work as you read this book. The next time you are visiting your bank, buy two or three rolls of pennies. When you get home, check the dates. The pre-1982 pennies were all made of copper, while the pennies minted after 1983 are zinc with a copper coating. In my little community I am finding that when I make this test, it is running about 50/50 (half pre-1982, half post 1983). When you consider the millions and millions of pennies that were minted before 1982, and how rapidly they are quietly disappearing, it tends to be a little overwhelming. Yet it is just another confirmation that Gresham's Law cannot be repealed, even by the lowly penny. Just for your information, I made my little test yesterday, and the ratio on two rolls of pennies was 25/75. Was it just a fluke, or is Gresham's Law working to its logical conclusion? You decide!

If you can accept the premise that economic laws are just as strong as physical laws, and if a physical law works as well on a small scale as it does on a large scale, then the same must hold true for economic laws. (I have also come to the conclusion that the same deduction can be made concerning spiritual laws, too, but that would take another entire book.) In an attempt to explain what the government is doing on a massive scale, I am going to give you an example of inflation on a very small scale. See if you think there is any correlation.

Let's pretend we are at an auction. There are 50 of us at this auction, and we all have various amounts of cash in our pockets. Each of us has worked hard for this money. Some of us have been more successful than others and have more cash in our pockets. Others of us have been just plain lucky, like farmer Brown whose family has worked the same patch of rocky ground for three generations, and oil was discovered on it last month. Now, this auction is

Chapter 2

strictly on a cash basis. We can't write checks, no credit cards, no running to the bank for more cash. Let's pretend that I have $1,000 and this is the most cash that any one person has in his pocket.

The auction starts, and various items go on the block. Then it happens -- a beautiful antique double barrel shotgun comes on the block. I hear music start to play, and I imagine that shotgun as my own. With trepidation in my heart, I start to bid. To my surprise, 20 of the people don't even bid (they are vegetarians). Another 20 don't bid because they think hunting is barbaric. The remaining ten of us start to bid --$100, $150, $300 (what will my wife think? She would rather have that pretty couch that is coming up for bid next, but I *must* have that shotgun). Higher and higher the bid goes -- $500, $750. Now only Mr. Smith, Farmer Brown and I are bidding on the shotgun. Mr Smith drops out at $800 -- he's simply run out of money. Although I don't know it, Farmer Brown only has $900 with him. He can't get any more cash, and I, in a frenzy, make my final bid --ONE THOUSAND DOLLARS!! The shotgun is almost mine! I can see myself making incredible shots with it! I am the envy of all my hunting companions! Going, going -- but wait, from the back of the room comes another bid from Mr. Smith. $1,100. Going, going, SOLD to Mr. Smith for $1,100. I am crushed. I wanted that shotgun. Oh, well. Guess I'll just bid on that couch for my wife.

It is only after the auction is over that I discover that Mr. Smith is a COUNTERFEITER! Not only is Mr. Smith a counterfeiter, but he cheated as well. When the bidding went past $800, he sent his assistant out to get more counterfeit currency, and was able to buy the shotgun. Now I want to ask you a question. Who was hurt by Mr.

Smith's counterfeiting? I want you to think about your answer before you read on.

The answer is *everyone who was at the auction!* Not only did I not get the shotgun, but the price of everything else at the auction is now raised by the amount of counterfeit money that Mr. Smith brought to the auction. If another bidder wants the couch and only has $300 in his pocket, I can still get the couch by topping his bid, simply because I have the $1,000 and I *didn't* spend on the shotgun. The rest of us had to work and save to get the money to bring to the auction, but Mr. Smith's only effort was to print up the money.

How do you feel about Mr. Smith's action? Don't you think that in addition to being a counterfeiter, he is also a thief? He stole my shotgun from me! He also stole the couch from the bidder who only had $300 because if I could have bought the shotgun, I wouldn't have had enough money to have bought the couch. He actually stole $1,100 from the 50 people that were at the auction, didn't he? In fact, he increased the cost of *every item being auctioned off.*

What if Mr. Smith wasn't Mr. Smith, but was actually a representative of our friendly and benevolent government – who wanted to purchase the shotgun for a poor widow lady who was dying of cancer, only had one leg, fourteen children, and wanted to be able to shoot a goose for Christmas dinner? Would he still be a counterfeiter and a thief?

What if the shotgun was needed for national defense? Would that fact change the effect of the counterfeit money on the rest of the bidders? Remember this simplistic example the next time you hear a politician blaming the Arabs or any other "bad boy" for the increase in the inflation rate. The inflation in this country comes from one source —our own government, aided and abetted by the Federal Reserve System and the fractional reserve banking system. If anyone tries to tell you that an increase in the price of gasoline, or bread, or even shotguns is the *cause* of inflation, put your hand on your wallet and quietly sneak toward the door. Either he doesn't understand economics, doesn't have a dictionary or is pointing a finger at a nonexistent "dragon" so that the blame won't be placed on him.

This book is not intended to be an economic text. If you have questions about inflation, money, credit, or why, if the price of gasoline goes up, it's not inflationary, read some books by the authors I mentioned earlier. I highly recommend "Common Sense Economics" by John A. Pugsley. Although I personally don't agree with some of his investment advice, his first chapter "Money, Government and You" is a classic.

Why is this brief discussion of inflation important? I personally feel the government will continue to use inflation as a method of paying its bills and supporting its huge defense and social welfare programs, and as inflation gets worse, life in the country is going to become more appealing.

In an effort to make your day complete, I would point out that there has never, in all of recorded history, been an inflationary boom that did not end in a terrible bust. In the 1790's, France experienced a terrible inflation, and the end result was Napoleon. For a complete economic history of that terrible period, read "Fiat Money Inflation in France", by Andrew Dickson White. The parallels with our economy today are frightening.

In the late 1920's, Germany experienced a hyper-inflation that our parents can still remember. It took literally bushels of currency to purchase a loaf of bread and the entire German economy ground to a halt. Another politician arose out of this morass of inflation and wage and price controls -- Adolf Hitler. Any good economic/history book on that period will tell you what happened, and why. For an interesting look at what investments worked during that period, try to get a copy of the pamphlet "The Nightmare German Inflation", published by Scientific Market Analysis, Princeton, New Jersey.

If inflation continues in this country at today's rate (as I write this book, the inflation rate is under 5%), then prices will *double* in approximately 14.5 years. The American people feel that inflation is now under control, and seem to feel confident about the future. I should point out that President Nixon slapped on wage and price controls when the inflation rate was approximately what it is today, and the people in power cheered the move as a sign "that someone was at last, doing something!" If the inflation rate goes up to 10%, then prices will double in approximately 7.2 years. To determine the number of years that it will take for prices to double, simply divide the number 72 by the rate of inflation (72 divided by 10% inflation equals 7.2 years). Don't ask me how this "Rule of 72" works. All that I know is that it does! But then, I don't understand how Gresham's Law works, either, only that it does.

If we make the assumption that inflation will continue in this country, then certain historical results can be anticipated. If we study some of the past inflations, we can get some reasonable ideas of what the future holds for us. First of all, long term credit in the form of fixed rate mort-

Chapter 2   15

gages and bonds will dry up. As it becomes more difficult for lenders to predict the future, the interest rates will reflect this uncertainty, and lenders will not want to loan their funds out over a long period of time. This drying up of long-term funds will cut down on your mobility, simply because it will be more difficult to buy and sell homes. If you can't sell your home in the city, it will be more difficult to move to the country.

Secondly, people on fixed incomes will be destroyed financially. As inflation increases, it will be impossible for the government to raise Social Security payments fast enough to keep up with the cost of living. If government tries to keep the increases coming, then the taxpayers (the young) will rebel. If the government doesn't keep the increases coming, then social security recipients (the old) will rebel. It makes no difference how the problem is finally resolved, someone is going to be mad, and someone is going to have the blame placed on them, probably by someone from our friendly, benevolent government. If you or your parents are depending on some form of annuity or pension plan from your employers, you had better take a long, hard look at it, because the odds are that it either won't be there when you need it, or the payments will be so small, based on today's purchasing power, that it won't buy much.

Thirdly, massive wealth transfers will take place. As people on the lower end of the economic scale find that they are making more and more money, but that it is buying less and less, they are going to be upset. Since only a handful of people in *any* economic class really understand what causes inflation, scape goats will have to be found. Probably our friendly, benevolent government will help us find these scape goats, assisted by their friends on the evening news and on the editorial pages of the newspaper. Some likely candidates are: the Arabs, Big Business, Labor Unions, and those unpatriotic people who are going against the public good by purchasing those barbaric, "non-productive" metals, silver and gold.

The rich will be blamed for more and more of the problems as *envy* starts to stalk the land. The "have nots" will start to envy the "haves" as their ability to cope financially is taken away from them, along with the hope of a better life for them and their children. They will have to blame someone for their plight, and historically, it has always been the people who are better off than they are. "If the rich man has it, he must have stolen it. Therefore, it's alright if I steal from him. Oh, I'm really not a thief, but the government really *should* take a portion of his wealth away to help those poor unfortunates who are worse off than I am."

And so it will go. We will be treated to interviews of politicians on the evening news will berate businesses for their "obscene profits", unpatriotic investors who insist on the right to invest in those barbaric metals, silver and gold, and "the rich" who just aren't paying their "fair share" of taxes. Big corporations will be blamed, and taxed even more, because only a few people understand that corporations don't PAY taxes, they only COLLECT the tax from their customers, and pass the tax along in the form of higher prices. Already, some misguided ministers are writing books advocating a "progressive tithe", with the government taking everything that you earn above $28,000 per year! Not only is it a dumb idea economically, the idea has no scriptural base.

As the times get worse, there will be more and more schemes to punish the producers and subsidize the nonproducers. Most of these schemes will be based on guilt and on envy. It may come as a shock to you, but before the inflationary cycle has run its course, *YOU* are going to be considered one of the rich if you are not receiving some sort of government support! The people who do not understand inflation are going to demand that some sort of punitive action be taken against those who do, so in the future, it will pay to keep your principles visible, and your assets invisible.

A fourth problem will occur as the division of labor starts to *decrease*. One of the inevitable results of inflation is a decrease in the division of labor. As the inflation rate soars, it will become less profitable to concentrate solely on your own profession, and you will find yourself making more repairs on automobiles and appliances, watching more television rather than going to movies, making do with older clothes. In short, doing more things for yourself that you would normally hire done. As inflation increases, the average man will find himself spending more and more of his take-home income on the staples of life, and less and less on the luxuries. On the other hand, the wealthy will be purchasing more Rolls Royces, antique paintings and works of art in an attempt to preserve their wealth and standard of living. This will inevitably lead to envy by the people that are struggling to get by, and laws will be demanded to make the "pain level" fair or equal (an utter impossibility).

If the inflation rates soar, we will become a nation of speculators. Instead of making investments that are future oriented, we will be forced to speculate on everything from commodities to rare coins in an attempt to preserve our remaining wealth. Greed will increase as people want the thing that they have pinned their hopes on to increase in value. Ultimately, if inflation runs its full course, and our currency becomes worthless through hyper-inflation, farmers will be trading sacks of potatoes for pianos as the process reverses itself and the collectibles become worth only what they will bring in a trade for staples. Very few people will understand what is actually happening to them, and as all of their attempts to maintain their status quo fail, they will want someone to blame. In France in the 1790's, it was the aristocracy that was blamed. In Germany in the 1920's, it was the Jews who were blamed for their nation's ills. In Cambodia in the 1970's, when the communists took over, it was anyone who wore glasses (they were considered to be "intellectuals").

As the pain of inflation increases, all sorts of rules, regulations and penalties will be imposed by our friendly, benevolent government in an attempt to keep the prices of products down. In France, in the 1790's it became a crime punishable by death to refuse to take the assignats (their dollar) that the government was printing in return for goods and services. With that law in place, the obvious happened, and the shopkeepers and tradesmen just took their products off the market, and there were no products for sale. Then the French government made it a capital offense to hoard goods or to refuse to perform services, and that further decreased the amount of goods and services that found their way to the market place. Even the black market dried up because the penalties for breaking the laws were so harsh, and many of the poor simply starved to death because there was no food available at any price.

Now I have no idea what the final outcome of inflation in our Country will actually be. All I can do is point out historically what has happened when a nation resorts to inflation in an attempt to be all things to all people, and give you a book list to read that will give you a historical basis for making your own decision. As bad as things are now in the cities, with crime, and smog, and frustration, and a decline in the quality of life, doesn't it really make a lot of sense to move to a quiet rural area where you will know your neighbors, and who can be trusted? Wouldn't you rather live in a small community where you can grow your own garden if you have to, and not worry about your produce being stolen from you? Wouldn't you really rather live in an area where you will be able to walk downtown without fear, and your children will still be able to attend a school without armed guards in the hallways? Life in a small community may have its problems if inflation runs its ugly course, but life there will be far better than in the cities. Here is a thought for you –If the worst does occur and you have moved you and yours to the safety of a small town, your life will still be better than any place in the *world* in the 1900's. Think about it.

Will It Be Deflation? Probably not. However, deflation could occur if one or two of our major banks failed, and the government couldn't shore them up quickly enough. I view this as a very limited possibility, simply because of all the *practice* that the government has had lately. In 1983, more banks failed than during the "Great Depression", and the public's reaction was a gigantic yawn. The FDIC program has obviously lessened the public's fear of bank failures.

Another event that would lead to a deflation is a massive repudiation of debt by the Third World Countries. If this occurred, and nothing were done about it, yes, a depression would wipe out the banking system. However, I have observed that every time a Third World Country starts hinting that it might be forced to repudiate its debt, some bank immediatly rushes to the rescue with a bigger loan so that the interest can be paid. My best guess is that if these massive debts *were* repudiated, the government would simply make it worth the effort of the debtor nations to trade their debt instruments for some sort of United States government bonds, and the entire debt would be monetized, and the privilege of paying these bonds off would be given to the American taxpayer. The ultimate result of this scenario would be inflationary, not deflationary.

Deflation could also occur by government design as it did in 1929 when the Federal Reserve System contracted the money supply by almost 25% overnight. For a complete history of this tragic period, I highly recommend "America's Great Depression" by Murray Rothbard. If you think that the depression was a "failure of capitalism", you have been sadly misled.

A nuclear war, even a limited one, could cause a deflation and resulting depression. But the social upheavals would be so great that the deflation or inflation of our money supply would be the least of our worries! It would only take one nuclear round on any major Western city to completely paralyze the banking system. If you were not able to write a check to purchase goods and services, the money supply would immediately shrink, and a deflation would result. Currency would be King, but I'm afraid that the man who sold a case of freeze-dried food for $3,000 in cash would be the ultimate loser. The value of currency might even increase if the printing presses were destroyed and the government couldn't print any more currency, but I wouldn't stake my investment future on that scenario.

I realize that there are several financial advisors that state over and over again that we are going to suffer a serious deflation and resulting depression, but all the evidence that I have seen indicates just the opposite. All of the economic evidence, and all of the historical information that I have read points to more inflation ahead, not deflation. But let's assume that I am wrong. Let's assume that by some quirk of fate a great deflation does occur. Will it be just like the depression of the 1930's? do you think that there will be long, quiet lines of men waiting for a meal? Do you think that large numbers of God-fearing families will be loading up their worldly possessions and heading for California in search of *jobs*? Are you hoping that your roll of pre-1964 dimes will enable you to buy a little farm somewhere? All the evidence that I have seen indicates, to me at least, that if we *do* suffer a deflation, the results will be far worse than anything that was recorded in the 1930's.

In New York City, the electricity went off for about 24 hours. During that time, there was looting, numerous fires were started, raping and pillaging occurred. Now you tell me -- if we have a deflationary depression, do you think these same people will quietly stand in line for a bowl of soup? If you have read "The Grapes of Wrath" by John Steinbeck, do you think that modern families will not blame anyone, but will just load up their families in pickups, and head for where they think they can find work?

First of all, the majority of modern families are broken homes, and secondly, they will be trying to leave the *city* in an attempt to get to the *country* where at least some food will be available. And what about those silver dimes that you have been carefully saving? All you have to do is make it to the country, and some bumpkin will sell you his house and forty acres for a couple of silver dimes! Forget it! A valuable economic asset, such as a farm, will continue to be a valuable economic asset, and you are not going to pick it up at a deep discount. The same would apply to food. Sure, you'll be able to pick up new cars for your silver dimes, because there won't be any gasoline to run them, but the necessities will be more expensive than they are today, simply because they won't be as readily available as they are now.

Your silver dimes will insure you a place in line, and a *chance* to acquire the tools of your trade, but please don't think that you are going to pick up valuable economic assets for virtually nothing. It simply won't happen.

Now having considered all of these factors, wouldn't you really rather live in the country? Wouldn't you rather live in an area where the people know you, and who would trade with you rather than with a stranger? Where you could still educate your children, and would have less fear about walking down town, even at night? Where you can grow your own food if you have to, and won't have to worry about someone stealing it from you? If a deflation occurs, it will be *this type of environment that a large number of people in the cities will be trying to get to!* Think about it.

Will It Be Wage and Price Controls? Predicting the future is a difficult task at best, but I think that if we look historically at what nations have tried in the past, we can make certain observations about the future. I have come to the conclusion that the "powers that be" in government have made a conscious decision to inflate the money supply. I have also come to the conclusion that the men at the highest levels of government are not dumb. They understand that if inflation continues to its logical conclusion, hyper-inflation will be the result. They have read some of the same books that I have suggested for you to read, and they know that if hyper-inflation does occur, the government in power will be wiped out in disgrace. They also know the free market will be left intact after the nightmare of hyper-inflation is over, and the government's ability to control its subjects will be greatly reduced. And that, dear reader, is what governments desire above all else, *CONTROL*.

The men in our government are finite men, just as we are, but they covet the power of the Infinite. They want to be able to direct the activity of other men, even when they can't find purpose and direction in their *own* lives. Look around you and honestly ask yourself, if a calamity of some kind occurs, will the government help the individual, or will it use the opportunity to strengthen its control over the individuals involved? Look at Aid To Dependent Children, food stamps, social security, disaster relief -- the list could go on and on. All of these programs were designed with the best of intentions, but they have all become major bureaucratic power centers, where the emphasis is not on helping people, but on acquiring "power" so that next year, the budget can be increased because of the "obvious need".

I have come to the conclusion that our government has learned to do one thing very well, and that is *to inflate the money supply* while, at the same time, pointing its finger at the *result* of this inflation, namely higher prices. It is my opinion that the government will continue this fiction as long as possible, and will then resort to wage and price controls in a misguided effort to slow the rise in prices. Earlier in this book, I mentioned that President Nixon invoked wage and price controls when the inflation level was at approximately the same place it is today. This move was greeted with applause by consumer advocates, career bureaucrats and many business men (who of all people, should have known better!) as an example of government finally "doing something".

Not long after the wage and price controls were placed in effect, we were treated to pictures of farmers in California drowning thousands of baby chicks, because it was going to cost more to raise them than they would bring in the market place under wage and price controls. We were shown pictures of people standing in line to buy a rationed amount of certain commodities because at the controlled price, there was more demand for a fixed amount of the product. We were told that there was a possibility that gasoline might have to be rationed, and that the oil companies were "bad boys", and were earning "obscene profits". It suddenly dawned on the American public that it was better to have all the gasoline that they wanted for $1.00 per gallon than it was to stand in line and get a rationed amount of gasoline at $.75 a gallon.

Now here is a thought for you -- wage and price controls don't control wages and prices! They control PEOPLE! Have you ever heard of a wage or a price being fined, or put in jail? Wage and price controls appeal to the bureaucratic mind because: 1. they give the appearance that you are "doing something", 2. they give an opportunity to expand the power base, 3. a missionary zeal can be given to the task, because "I'm doing something *important*", and 4. it gives the enforcer of the rules a feeling of power and importance (I'm sorry, Mrs. Jones, the rules say you can only have one jar of peanut butter. After all, we must be fair to the people who are in line behind you!). If wage and price controls are placed on the American public again (and I'm certain that they will be), do you think that it will be easier to control the people in the cities, or in the country?

One, or a combination of, the three scenarios outlined

above *will* occur some time in the future. Regardless of which scenario occurs, wouldn't you really rather live in a small, attractive rural community, where you know your neighbors and they know you? A place where you will be able to walk down town without fear and send your children to school with the assurance that they will get an education and won't be mugged? A place where you can work out a deal with a mechanic you trust that will get your car fixed, regardless of whether the "fixing" agrees with some nebulous government regulation? A place where, if you really had to, you could raise a garden, and not worry about your produce being stolen? Don't you think that you owe it to yourself and your family to move to an area of relative calm as the storm clouds build on the horizon?

Chapter 3

Preparing For The Move

Picking the Place. It is beyond the scope of this book to rate small towns for you. Most of you have already seen a small community that appeals to you, and would move there in a minute if you "could just figure out how to make a living there!" As the title of this book indicates, you will be given loads of information on how to earn a living in a small community (I'll guarantee that many of the ideas you will receive will be entirely new to you, plus I'll give you some new ideas for doing old, well known jobs differently). For those of you who have not, as yet, picked out YOUR town, I would make these suggestions to you.

First, sit down with your family and decide what area of the country you would prefer to live in if you had all the money in the world. This important, because if your spouse "hates the desert", it makes absolutely no sense to plan on moving there. If you love the mountains, then get an Atlas, and start looking for small rural communities in the mountains of your choice. If you enjoy the seashore, then pick the coast that you prefer, and start writing down the names of small towns. As you actually start looking at the map and writing down the names of towns, you will automatically start to eliminate some of them.

Second, when you have narrowed the choice down to

several that look good, write to their Chamber of Commerce. If they don't have one, write to the principal of the school system, the minister of your denomination or to the police department, and just tell them that you are planning to move to their community, and to give you all the information they can about their community. You could even make out a list of questions that concern you, and ask them to give you their opinion on these items. The town that I live in has a very active Chamber of Commerce, and every month they receive dozens of requests for information, and mail out packets of information on the area. I'm sure other towns do the same. When you get this information, *study it!* If you have only visited the mountains in the summer, it may come as a shock to you that it gets cold in the winter, and that sometimes the snow can cover the fences. Try to eliminate all of the negative surprises.

Third, visit the towns that you have picked. Do it this weekend if they are close enough. If not, take some time off from your work, and do it next week, but make up your mind that this move you are making is vitally important (which it is), and deserves special effort on your part (which it does). When you arrive at the towns of your choice, have a check list of things that are important to you, and check these things out. One of the first areas we checked was the Churches. You can get a good idea of how the community feels about itself by finding out how it feels about its Creator. Since we had small children, we always checked out the school system. If the buildings are well maintained, you have an idea of how the people feel about education. If you can find a teacher, especially at the high school, ask a lot of questions. What are the school system's strong points/weak points? How many of the graduates go on to college? How many scholarships were awarded to seniors last year? Do any of the graduates go on to service academies -- the list should include the things that are important to YOU. Go to the local bank, and ask to speak to one of the officers. Ask quesions. Tell him what you are doing, and ask for advice. People love to talk, especially about their community. Get all of the information you can, and then go home and digest it.

When my wife and I decided to move to a small town, we had already picked out the area that we preferred. We hooked up a travel trailer, and spent two weeks driving through, and checking out, the small mountain communities we had chosen. We systematically eliminated all of the communities we visited until we came to our next-to-the-last-stop-- and we fell in love with "our" little town. Two days later, we bought our current house, and six weeks later, we had wrapped up our affairs in the city, and moved to our little country town. I thought we were unique until we started meeting some of our neighbors. One friend, an attorney worked as a security guard in Denver until he found the job he wanted here. He now owns the business that hired him. Another friend, who with his wife and two small children, lived in a travel trailer here until he found the job that he wanted. Another acquaintance had a small, independent income, and moved here because he loved to fish. He now fishes full time, and sells real estate part time. Another fellow who was tired of New York City, was driving through, and saw a camera shop for sale. He bought it, and has never regretted his move. "T" was a student at our local college. He fell in love with the area, and didn't want to leave after graduation. He now has a small, but successful contracting firm. A young couple was traveling through the area, and fell in love with it. They went home, and figured out that the community needed a "one hour" photograph shop.

They sold their house, purchased the necessary equipment, and moved out here, and are doing a great business. The list could go on and on. Probably 30% of my good friends here just decided this is where they wanted to live, and proceeded to make their dreams come true. Can you do the same? Certainly you can! All it takes is a lot of "want to" and a little bit of planning.

Planning The Move. After selecting "your" little town, you have a lot of work ahead of you. If you are a professional, you have to sell your current practice, and prepare for your new one. If you own a small business, you must either sell it, or figure out how to move it to your new home. If you are like the majority of Americans, and work for a salary, then you must decide how you are going to support your family when you arrive at your new home. The last half of this book is filled with actual case histories of people just like you that have left salaried jobs in the city, and have made it on their own in the country. They are no different than you are – they just set a goal for themselves, and DID IT!

A good rule of thumb would be to have enough cash to live modestly for a period of six months without a job of any kind. Although I have known people that have moved with less than $100 in their pockets, and have been very successful, *my* nerves couldn't handle a situation like that. It is highly unlikely that it will take you six months to find a job or a business opportunity that appeals to you, but if you have this six month cushion, it will be a lot easier on your mental state. If you already own a home, then selling it may give you your "nest egg". You may already have enough savings, and may not have to worry about how to acquire this six month nest egg, but if you don't, here are some suggestions on how you can acquire this nest egg -- fast!

1. Start a systematic savings plan TODAY! You will be surprised at how much money is slipping through your fingers every month. A systematic savings plan will help you budget your available assets and enable you to save money you are now just frittering away. If you are like most of us, you will be shocked at the amount of money you spend on "junk" every month. This money can be saved, and applied to your goal of moving to the country.

2. Get a second job, either in the evenings, or on the weekends. Most of us think we have put in a rough week if we work 8 hours a day, five days a week. Yet half the world works longer than that just to put food on the table! If you can just work an extra 10 hours a week at the minimum wage, you could be earning and saving another $130.00 per month -- minimum! Use your wits, and try to figure out a way to beat the minimum wage. Use your own imagination, and the suggestions in this book, and see if you can figure out a part-time business that will make you that extra income today, and would be a business that you could use when you move to the country. Get the rest of the family involved. If they are as excited as you are about to move to the country (and they will be if you have included them in your planning), get them involved in making and saving money.

3. Sell the car. This may seem like a harsh statement, but it has been my observation that most families could live well just on what they spend each month on car payments, upkeep, and gasoline. If a car is a necessity in your work, get rid of the expensive behemoth in your driveway, and get a smaller, used car that will be less expensive to operate. If you don't already know how to per-

form minor maintenance, such as changing the oil, replacing the spark plugs, and checking the fluid levels –LEARN! It will not only save you money, but it will build your confidence level. If you think that a new car every three years is a necessity, it's time to change your way of thinking. Besides, when you get to your new country home, you will probably discover that your neighbors could "care less' about what kind of car you drive, and are much more interested in what kind of a person you are. Give this money saving idea some serious thought.

4. Have a Garage Sale. In different parts of the country, they are known by different names -- yard sales, white elephant sales, junk sales -- but by what ever name they are called, they can be very successful. When my wife and I moved here, we made enough money from a garage sale to pay for the services of a commercial mover. We probably could have saved another $800 if we had rented a truck and moved everything ourselves, but I HATE moving!

You will be surprised -- nay, *shocked* at what people will buy at these sales. When you are getting ready to move, don't throw away anything -- just save it for your garage sale. Someone will buy it, I promise. There was an elderly couple in our community that made a good living just attending garage sales. They would go to every garage sale they could find, and "cherry pick" the sale. They would buy items that they knew were under-priced, and then, once a month, have a garage sale of their own. He told me that they made more than their social security check each month, just by spending a few hours attending garage sales. I don't know what happened to this old couple, they moved away several years ago, but this funny old man gave me a secret that made him a good living over a long period of time. He gave me two "secret" phrases with which he supported his wife, and made his life easier. I have used these two "secret" phrases, myself, and I can assure you that they work. *If you will use them, these two phrases are worth ten time the price you paid for this book!*

The two phrases are *"What wouldja take"* and *"wouldja take"*. Don't laugh, and don't feel misled. These two phrases made this old man a good living. When I have used them property, and more importantly, understood the power that they contain, I have made literally thousands of dollars! But let me tell you how this old "master" used them. As I told you, he made a good living, just attending garage sales. He would pick out some special "treasure", look at the price, and then take it to the person in charge. Let's say the "treasure" was marked $10.00. With sorrowful eyes, he would look at the person, and say the first secret phrase, "What wouldja take for this?" The person, not knowing he was receiving a college-level education in economics, would invariably reply, "Oh, $7.50." (The old "master" just made 25%.) The old man would then reach in a frayed pocket of his faded overalls, and produce a coin purse that looked like moths should fly out of it when he opened it. He would reach in his old coin purse, and, with trembling fingers, take out a five dollar bill, and repeat the second secret phrase "wouldja take $5.00 for it?" The answer was invariably "Yes", and the old "master" had just made a 50% savings, just because he knew these two secret phrases!

By using these techniques, this old man was almost always able to receive a price reduction. If he didn't, he wouldn't buy the item. He also used this same tactic with damaged goods -- in supermarkets and department stores, of all places! He told me that he was successful in getting a price reduction more than 50% of the time.

Now this old man and his wife were a funny looking couple, and I'm convinced that they had never heard of Ludwig von Mises or Henry Hazlitt, but I'm also convinced that they knew more about free market economics than most college professors! I asked him once, what he would do if someone tried these two secret phrases on *him*. He told me, with a twinkle in his eye, "I jus'put a sad look on my face, and sez NO."

When I have used these two secret phrases properly, I have saved literally thousands of dollars purchasing real estate and cars. Don't just take these two phrases at face value, but study them, and you will learn more about human nature (economics) than you ever dreamed possible.

5. Cut out the luxuries. There are many areas of your life that are expensive, and unnecessary. If you are serious about making your move to the country, you can speed up this move simply by eliminating or reducing some of your luxuries. If you eat lunch out every day, start "brown-bagging it". If you have been spending $5 to $10 on lunch, you can save between $100 and $200 per month. If you have been stopping in the evening to "have one with the boys (girls)", cut it out, and you'll save another $100 per month. If you are a smoker, quit. Not only will you save $18 to $25 per month, your health will improve. If you have been dropping $20 to $30 to go to the movies, stay at home and watch reruns -- it's essentially the same pap. Better yet, spend the time at your public library studying about the town and area you have picked. Check the business section for ideas on jobs and businesses you might start when you get to your new country home. In short, make more productive use of your most valuable economic asset: TIME.

The "experts" tell me that approximately 90% of the

people who read this book will become excited at the prospects of moving to the country, will think about it for a few days, and then will forget the whole thing. All of the familiar excuses will be trotted out -- I can't save enough money, my family will have to leave all of their friends, my job is secure and I may not be able to find another one, I may not like it, and will have wasted time and capital -- you can add YOUR excuse to the list. It seems to me that the reasons for *not* making the move can really be reduced to *1. a lack of motivation,* and *2. fear of the unknown.*

If you lack motivation, read some of the books that I have suggested to you. Think out the problem. Try to find some current articles on what is happening in Israel (inflation rate over 400%) and Brazil (inflation rate over 120%). Try to understand what is happening to *their* economies, and you will get a good idea of what will happen to ours. Think the next few years through logically, and see if you really do want to be living where you are now if the worst does occur.

Pick out the rural community that you want to make your home, and then start dreaming about it. See yourself living there, having a good time. If you enjoy fishing, then imagine yourself fishing on a Thursday afternoon. If you enjoy skiing, then imagine you and your family skiing on the weekend. If you enjoy picnics, imagine yourself picnicing by a babbling brook with no one near you to disturb the beauty of the setting.

Let me ask you a question -- if you *don't* take the advice of this book, and start planning your move to the country, what will you be doing in two years, three years, five years? Will the move be easier then than it is now? Will your children be better off then than they are now? Will you be happier then than you are now? If the answer is *no*, then why put the move off any longer than necessary? Procrastination is the great killer of dreams, so why procrastinate?

Fear of the unknown is probably the greatest fear that mankind suffers. I wish I could remember who said it, but somewhere in my youth, I remember a wise old man saying "90% of the things I worried about in my life never happened." Think about that statement for a second. If 90% of the things you worry about never occur, then you've wasted a lot of time worrying over nothing! If you are worried about "what my friends will say," they will probably tell you that they have dreamed of doing what you are doing. If they haven't, so what! When you make your move, I'll bet you that your best friends will visit you in less than six months, and then give you a list of "reasons" why they can't move. Do you fear failure? So what? Most of life's successful people have failed at *something* in their life! If you continue to look at only the negative, then you will miss out on all of the good positive things that could have happened.

In all of the small rural communities that I have visited, I have *never* seen anyone that was visibly starving to death, nor have I seen anyone in stocks on the Town Square with the word "FAILURE" written over his head. The opportunities are there — all you have to do is open yourself up to them and work! Let me share one of my favorite poems with you. This was written by Jessie B. Rittenhouse, from "The Door of Dreams, Houghton, Mifflin & Co., Boston":

"I bargained with Life for a penny,
And Life would pay no more,
However I begged at evening
When I counted my scanty store.

"For Life is a just employer:
He gives you what you ask,
But once you have set the wages,
Why, you must bear the task.

"I worked for a menial's hire,
Only to learn, dismayed,
That any wage I had asked of Life,
Life would have willingly paid."

It's up to you. In six months or less, you can be living your dream in the country home of your choice -- or you can be doing exactly what you are today. The decision is yours.

Chapter 4

Earning A Living In The Country

Getting a Job. Getting a job in the country is going to be a little different from what you are used to in the city. First of all, unless you have a trade or skill that someone in your town is desperate for, the odds are that the person hiring you is going to want to know you for a while before you are hired. If you are planning your move to a resort area, this is even more of a probability because in resort areas, employers are accustomed to people falling in love with the area, and applying for a job, only to never show up for work, or leave after the "season" is over. In the city, your employer is going to be more interested in what your qualifications are. In the country, your employer is going to be more concerned with what kind of *person* you are.

It has been my observation that the most successful way to land a job in a small community is to move there first, and find a job second -- just the opposite of what a normal job seeker would do. If you have saved your nest egg as I outlined in the previous chapter, I would advise you to move to the community of your choice, rent a house or apartment, and just enjoy yourself for a week or two. Join the Church of your choice, attend what ever service club you were a member of in the city, in short, start introducing yourself into the social fabric of the community. Take part in any community service that you can find, and try to make yourself as visible as possible. Every time someone asks you the inevitable question "What do you do for a living", (and believe me, they will), tell them! If you are looking for a job, ask for suggestions. Ask them if they know anyone in your field that needs help. As the people in your chosen community become more at ease with you, your chances of finding the job you want will also become easier.

There is a definite feeling of "we take care of our own" in a small community, and if you are already living in the community, this concern for others will work to your benefit. If you have followed my advice, there is no reason to panic. You have enough money in your nest egg to live comfortably for up to six months, so you can take your time, and find a job that you really enjoy. I should point out that you very well may be "under-employed" for a while. By that, I mean that you may find it necessary to take a job that is beneath your ability level and educational level. In a small town, it is not unusual to find college graduates working as clerks in a store or performing menial tasks. It is also not unusual to find high school graduates (or dropouts) owning some of the major businesses in your community. *What matters is your ability to find a need, and then fill it, not how much education you have acquired.* If you feel that it is somehow "beneath you" to take a menial job, or to work at a task that does not require any education, then maybe you need to adjust your thinking. If you find yourself in a situation such as this, use the menial job to prove your worth. Be so prompt and helpful and cheerful that you are noticed. If you will take advantage of your opportunities, I will assure you that even more opportunities will come your way!

Chapter 4

If You Are A Professional. If you are trained as a lawyer, Certified Public Accountant, doctor, nurse, or have training in any profession, you are in luck. These skills are in great demand in a small community, and you will be welcomed with open arms. These types of services are as needed in the country as they are in the city, and believe me, your clients and patients will be much more appreciative than those you have been working with in the city. Just make sure that you are not *too* specialized. Remember my previous example about the brain surgeon and the general practitioner -- the smaller population base may make it harder to find enough "customers" in a small town.

As a professional, it will be easier for you to make a "lot of money" in the city, but are you aware of the personal costs of such a decision? If you die at the age of 42 with a stress induced heart attack, what good will all the money you made be? In a small community, you will be able to make a good living, and will have the respect of the members of your community.

Buying An Existing Business. My experience in buying an existing business was a bad one, so my judgment on this subject may very well be clouded. Let me tell you the mistakes that I made, so you will be aware of what *not* to do. I purchased one of the oldest, most established businesses in my community. I paid too much for the "blue sky" or goodwill that the business supposedly had. I also purchased a lot of real estate with the business, meaning that I had a lot of debt to service on a monthly basis. My location was superb, but parking was limited, reducing the number of drop-in customers. My timing was terrible -- I purchased this business just as our community entered a building recession that lasted for three years. Never in my life had I worked so hard, and made so little money. I was fortunate to sell the business back to its original owner -- for a fraction of what I paid for it! I paid off all of my creditors, and retreated to lick my wounds and figure out where I had gone wrong. Just so you will know, I was not inexperienced in business. My parents had owned a retail business, and I grew up in that environment, working with them. After a business degree in college, I worked for Dun & Bradstreet for almost three years, receiving an excellent education in why businesses succeed, and why they fail. I also worked for a major metropolitan bank, and dealt first-hand with small businesses. As you can see, I had an excellent background for going into business for myself, and still, I failed.

It was upsetting for me to see a good friend of mine put in a small sandwich shop, only be open for lunch, and make over three times what I was making! He would be home by 3:00 in the afternoons, and I was lucky to get home by 7:00 at night -- after starting at 6:00 in the morning! He generally made it to work between 10:30 and 11:00 in the mornings! It became apparent to me that I had made a mistake in purchasing the business I did, when I sold an old building that I had purchased a year earlier for more profit than I had made working my fingers to the bone for 18 months in my own business!

If you are contemplating the purchase of an existing business, my advice to you would be as follows:

1. AVOID DEBT LIKE THE PLAGUE!! It is easy to borrow money to go into business (especially from the previous owner), but it is difficult to pay it back, and still pay yourself a salary. My advice to you would be to only borrow money as a last resort, and then to worry about it constantly! Borrowing money to expand a successful operation that you have been running for a while is one thing, but borrowing money to purchase and run an

existing business can be the kiss of death.

2. BEWARE OF PAYING FOR "BLUE SKY", "GOODWILL", OR "A GOOD REPUTATION". The old expression, "you can't eat goodwill" is still a good one. It may appeal to you to purchase a going concern that has a trained staff, adequate inventory and a past history of operation, but why pay for an intangible that may be nonexistent in the first place, or may evaporate the first month you own the business? Spend your money on tangibles -- inventory, fixtures, labor saving macines, not on intangibles like goodwill.

3. BE EXTREMELY WARY ABOUT PURCHASING THE REAL ESTATE THAT CONTAINS THE BUSINESS YOU ARE BUYING. It is amazing, but in the four small communities that I have checked on in the past six months, business buildings in the main part of town were renting for between $400 and $700 per month. These same buildings could have been purchased for between $65,000 and $95,000. It makes absolutely no economic sense to purchase a building for $95,000 that you can rent for $700 a month! If you disregard this advice and buy a building, what are you going to do if a competitor comes in with a better location? Or if a new shopping center is started? Business buildings are sometimes difficult to sell, and you just don't need the headaches. Have an attorney draw up a lease that is air tight and as favorable to you as possible, and then spend the difference between what your monthly rent is, and what your monthly mortgage payment would have been! Avoid escalator clauses (especially those based on the Consumer Price Index) if at all possible. If you *must* sign a lease with an escalator clause, insist that the increase be stated in dollar amounts, and not in a percentage. If inflation soars in the future, an escalator clause based on a percentage could kill you.

4. USE GOOD JUDGMENT. Be skeptical. If the previous owner tells you that his business actually makes much more than his business records show, *be careful*, because if he has been stealing from the IRS, he probably will have no qualms about stealing from you (or at least telling you a little fib). There is a touch of larceny in all of us, but we're talking about investing in a business. Don't let your dislike of the Internal Revenue Service cloud your good judgment. If the owner tells you his volume is $3 billion a month, park across the street, and spend a day counting the number of customers that walk in his door. Common sense will tell you if he is truthful or not. In a resort community just north of where I live, an accountant once laughingly told me, "the main business of this little town is selling businesses!" He was correct. None of the businesses being sold actually made any money -- they were just vehicles that people with some money were using so they could move to this beautiful resort community, and have an excuse for their move! If you have that kind of money, why buy a business in the first place!

5. JUST BECAUSE AN EXISTING BUSINESS IS A SUCCESS NOW IS NO GUARANTEE THAT IT WILL CONTINUE TO SUCCEED UNDER YOUR MANAGEMENT. People can have some funny ideas. I purchased a business that had been around since the 1890's, and had several people tell me that they hadn't come in my store because "it just didn't seem right" without the former owners there! You will always be compared with how "they" did things, and the human memory is notorious for forgetting the bad experiences and remembering only the good experiences.

In small communities, your personality is very important, and if your personality differs from the previous owner's, this can hurt your business. If the previous owner is having a bad day, the customer's response can be "I wonder what's wrong with him, he must be having a bad day!", but if YOU happen to be having a bad day, the response is often "this guy is a creep! It'll be a cold day before I come in here again!!". You get the point. In a small town, your customers don't just see a business, they look at the business as an extension of YOU, and if you are purchasing a business from a person or family that has been a part of the community for years, your customers may just not be able to make the transfer, and all of the merchandising skill in the world won't change this perception.

In most cases, the ideal situation may be to start a business of your own. This is not as hard as it sounds, and in many cases, may actually be cheaper than buying an existing business. Your best bet is to start a business that currently does not exist in your community, or if competition exists, is grossly mis-managed. We will concentrate on businesses that take a minimum of capital to start. After all, you want a business that will make you a nice income, but at the same time will allow you to take some time off, and enjoy your family and the area that you have chosen.

One final thought, be careful about starting any business in a small town that competes with an existing business. Although you may be successful, your chances of failure are increased, simply because of your competitor's established personality. Give this aspect some serious thought, especially if you have never lived in a small community before.

Chapter 5

Successful Country Businesses

This chapter is my favorite! Here you will read about small businesses that have made their owners RICH! Not just rich in money, but rich in the things that really count in life -- time to spend with their children, a satisfying lifestyle, time to pursue a hobby, time to share helping others. In every one of the examples I am about to give you, I can truthfully say that the people that I saw working at the job described were HAPPY! They were enjoying what they were doing, and were getting a "kick" out of life. With the exception of one old grouch who was too dumb to count his blessings, every one of these people was a person who I think YOU would have enjoyed meeting, too. Some of them were not making a lot of money, but they were rich in the things that really mattered. One man told me, "Charles, I could be making a lot more money if I were still living back in the city, but here, I've been able to carve out a living on my own. The security that that gives a man just can't be taken away from him. I get to see my kids when they get home from school, and I know my neighbors. Sure, I'd like to make a little more money, but heck, I'm richer than KINGS were a hundred years ago!"

Think about what he said, and I believe you will see the truth of his statement. He was more "secure" than any corporate employee, because he knew that even if he lost *everything*, he could just pick himself up, and start over again! Now *that's* security!

Now it should be obvious that not all of the examples I am going to give to you will be something that you will want to do, or for that matter, have the ability to do. But somewhere in this chapter, you *WILL* find something that appeals to you, and that fits your abilities. When you find it, write your OWN ideas and variations in the margins. Start to think about how YOU could do the same thing, only with a few of your personal ideas thrown in for good measure! The people that I saw working at these jobs were no different than you are. None of them were born rich, were "special", or had some secret that you don't have. What they DID have was a burning desire to live in the country, and fulfill their own dreams. If you don't think that *you* can do the same, you are selling one of God's finest creations short.

Let's get into it! It has been my observation that some of the most successful small town businesses revolve around FOOD! It seems that no matter how small the town, there is *always* room for a good restaurant that sells good (different) food, at a modest price while providing good service. The restaurant business can be a dreary 24 hour a day, 7 day a week business, or it can be a real joy – as these examples prove.

Example #1
Specialty Restaurant

I went to high school with "W", and I don't want to embarrass him, but he would be the first to admit that he did not graduate with honors, nor was he voted "Most Likely To Succeed". In fact, I think that he was the first member of his family to graduate from high school. This summer, I saw him for the first time in about 25 years, and he told me that he had gone "broke" trying to raise peanuts, and that, out of desperation, he had started his restaurant. His mother had a recipe for catfish and hushpuppies that would make the angels sing. He took this recipe, rented an old building on the highway, and started selling catfish dinners. Now the building was certainly nothing fancy, and the furnishings consisted of simple tables and chairs. Everything was served in a "basket", and if you insisted on silverware, they brought out the engraved stuff (marked "U.S."). He told me that he was only open from 5:00 to 9:00 in the evenings, THREE NIGHTS A WEEK! His mother and father took care of greeting people at the door and taking in the money. "W" and his wife were cooking in the kitchen, and his children waited on the tables -- a true family affair. Now I don't know how much money "W" was making, but he obviously was supporting three families well. He really enjoyed what he was doing, and he certainly had a lot of free time to fish and hunt. The evening that I was there, 26 people were in line ahead of us, just waiting to get in the door, and when we left at about 8:30, people were *still* waiting to get in! However you choose to define *success* in life, I think you would have to admit that "W" had obtained it.

Could you do something like this? Certainly you could!

If you have an old "family" recipe for catfish, barbecue, frog legs, chicken, calf fries or whatever, get it out and see if it is still as good as you remember it to be. If you like to cook, and don't have an old "family" recipe, check some cookbooks out of the library and study. Just because you're not Chinese doesn't mean that you can't cook good Chinese food. Then follow "W's" example – keep your opening costs as low as possible, have lots of parking, and make sure that the aroma of the food being cooked can be smelled while your customers are waiting in line. (I don't think he planned the last item that way, but it was *very* effective! By the time we got inside, we were so hungry that we ate TWO orders!) Keep your operating costs as low as possible, and pass the savings on to your customers in the form of modest prices. The repeat business will make you a very comfortable living.

Example #2
Sandwich Shop

"L" and his wife fell in love with the rocky mountains, and decided that they would like to stay in our area for a while. "L" was a sharp individual, and had a little capital, so he rented a small building with lots of parking and high visibility, and opened up a sandwich shop. He sold *good* corned beef, pastrami, roast beef, wurst and vegetarian sandwiches. He had a daily special, and always threw in a free pickle. He started out with an eye-level cooler for the soft drinks and a microwave oven. He had an unemployed carpenter build him a counter and three or four wooden booths so you could sit down if you felt you really had to. Later on, he added a long floor model cooler so his customers could see the various meats, cheeses and desserts. He usually had one or two college girls working for him, and they specialized in fast, friendly service, and would take telephone orders.

During the Christmas season, he put together and sold cheese baskets, and mailed them all over the country. If I remember correctly, he used to gripe because he was having to work 8 to 10 hours a day during this four week period! His normal hours were from 11:00 in the morning until 2:00 in the afternoon, six days a week. This small business enabled him to live very well, but more important, gave him the freedom that he valued so highly. He had trained his staff well, and when he and his wife wanted to take a little time off, they could be out of town, and the business would still be making money for them!

Could you do something like this? Sure you could! "L" just took a good idea that he had seen somewhere else, and moved it to HIS community. You could certainly do the same. This particular business has sold three times since "L" decided to move to California -- each time for a little more than the last. He made a good living while he owned the business, and then sold it for enough cash to "retire on" for a while.

Example #3
Restaurant With A View

I thought "J" was crazy when he built another restaurant in our little town. After all, we were in the midst of the worst economic recession in the past 30 years, and we had plenty of restaurants -- some of which were having a difficult time surviving. But he had an idea, and that idea has proven to be a moneymaker. Earlier, he had purchased a small strip commercial building right on the intersection of our two busiest downtown streets. Two of the businesses in the building were eateries, one of which he owned. He decided to build a large addition with lots of glass, and expand his restaurant. About this time, he had an opportunity to purchase another local business, and decided to lease his new location to another gentleman. The new restauranteur is doing a land office business. The food is great, and the portions are generous, and the service is excellent. The location is tops because people can walk from our downtown area. But the thing that packs the people in is the *glass*. If you are inside, you can watch people walking by and the traffic as it passes. If you are outside, you can see all of the customers enjoying a good meal.

The next time you are in a restaurant, see where most of the people want to be seated. I'll bet that most of them would like to be next to a window, so they can see out. "J's" idea was to make three entire walls a "window", and it has been an incredible success!

Could you do something like this? You would need more capital than the other two examples given above, and you would need a location that was similar to "J's", but sure you could. I am convinced that the large amount of glass is the main item responsible for the success of the business. A simple, little idea, but it is making two families a good income, and providing several others with jobs. And by the way, the restaurant is only open for breakfast and lunch!

Example #4
Donut Shop

If your small community doesn't have one, why not open a DONUT SHOP? Our community has two, and both seem to be doing well. As with any eatery, the most important factor seems to be the location. You must either be located in an area that has a lot of pedestrian traffic, or on a highly visible site with a lot of automobile traffic. If you are an early riser, this business is a natural for you. If you are going to open at 6:00 A.M., you will probably have to get to work at about 4:30 A.M., but you will be able to close at noon, so there are some advantages, as well.

There are several franchises available in this field, but you might be ahead to purchase your own equipment, and start your own donut business. The equipment to make donuts is readily available, and I can't imagine that there would be that much to learn. I'm sure that any good library would have dozens of cook books with enough donut recipes to keep you happily experimenting for weeks. If your lack of experience bothers you, why not quit your present job, and work for one of the large donut franchises for a while, and learn all that you can from them. Most of them stay open 24 hours a day. I'm not certain that those hours would be profitable in a small town, but you can experiment and find out what works for you.

My advice to you would be to pick a location that has plenty of parking, and is on your town's busiest street. Make sure that your location has plenty of windows, so that people can see out (and see in). Have a large area where people can sit and eat donuts while drinking their coffee. And one more thing, keep the place spotlessly clean!

Could you do something like this? If early hours don't bother you, sure you could! Just keep your opening expenses low, and your profit margin high. Produce a good product, and develop a gimmick -- free coffee, free donuts to ladies or children, give a "baker's dozen" (13 donuts when 12 are purchased), hire a teenager, and have him/her sell donuts directly to the people at the courthouse, and the downtown businesses. You get the idea, do something unusual, and get the "word of mouth" advertising going. People love good things to eat, and when someone says, "let's go get a cup of coffee", you want their first thought to be of you!

Example #5
Push Carts

If you choose a resort community to settle in, a good living can be made during the "season" by selling hot dogs, polish sausage and barbeque sandwiches from a cart. I'm not sure where you can buy the carts, but I'll bet any good restaurant magazine would have the information. Check in your local library. I've seen several of these carts in operation over the State, and they were always doing a good business. Be sure that you have the proper permits, and then just find where the crowds are! The models that I have seen were self-contained, and had their own heating systems. The aroma of sausages and hot mustard can carry for over a block, and it draws the customers like crazy!

I suspect that some of these "street corner entrepreneurs" follow the seasons, and move from place to place as the weather and tourist crowds shift. Because of what I believe the future holds, I do not recommend this type of existence, but if you have no family responsibilities and enjoy the life of a vagabond, this could be just the ticket for you. I have seen people selling helium filled balloons on piers, families selling home-made lemonade and limeades at hot county fairs, popcorn and hot pretzel stands -- all doing a thriving business. You could start out part-time on the weekends, and just see how things go, but again, I can't recommend this lifstyle to you.

I must confess to you that I don't have an "artsy-craftsy" bone in my body. In fact, one of my vivid memories of grade school is being tied for "last" in Mrs. Seeley's penmanship class. It took this other little fat kid and me the entire semester to pass the basic test, while the pretty little girls were able to pass the test, and get out of the class in four weeks! I always figured that Mrs. Seeley just passed the other kid and me just to get rid of us. I have always admired anyone that can paint a beautiful picture, or throw a piece of pottery, simply because I don't possess the talent.

If you have any artistic ability at all, you can make a living with your art -- if you know THE SECRET! THE SECRET is *not* how well you paint, or sculpt or carve, the secret lies in first, knowing what the common man perceives as art, and appealing to that perception, and second, and most important, KNOWING HOW TO SELL YOUR PRODUCT. Most of history's great painters died poor and unfulfilled, because the public did not perceive what they were producing as "art". If you want to start a new trend in art, or write the "great American novel", then I wish you well (and hope , for your sake, that you were born rich). If you are an average person, with an above average talent, then you *must* figure out what the majority of people find attractive, and then figure out a way to sell it in *large quantities*. You must go to art shows, wholesale gift shows, and if all else fails, go to individual gift stores in an attempt to market your product. This one point is where the majority of artists fail.

If you spend your waking hours making doillies out of crushed pine cones, and can't market them, you've wasted *your* time, not to mention a lot of pine cones! The following examples are people that I have actually known and observed making a living with their art, while living in the country. Let's face it – it's hard to be a painter of landscapes if you live in Chicago, or Los Angeles, or Gary, Indiana. If you want to paint and improve your talent, then what better way than to move to a beautiful area with breathtaking scenery? If you don't make the move this year, will you improve your talent where you are? Will you be any happier in two years, three years, five years? The choice is yours.

Example #6
Wood Turning

I know three people who earn money turning vases and bowls on a lathe. One of these people earns a living on a full time basis, and the other two supplement their incomes with their hobby. The difference between a full time job, and a part time hobby is *marketing*. The man who makes a full time living at this gets out and sells his product. He has an established route of gift stores, curio shops and wholesalers. He isn't afraid to get out, and knock on doors if necessary to sell his product. He has one or two people working for him, and can't seem to make the stuff fast enough!

If this idea appeals to you, I'll try to give you all the information I can. In this particular example, it is more important for you to have a working knowledge of tools than it is for you to be an artist. You will need a good wood turning lathe, and the proper hand-held tools for working on a lathe. All of the work that I have seen, used as its raw material dry aspen wood. Aspen is a soft wood, and is relatively easy to work with. I feel certain that any dry, thoroughly seasoned soft wood would work, but in the area where I live, aspen is available in large quantities, usually free for the taking (another good reason for living in the country -- have you priced a cord of firewood lately in YOUR community?). I don't know why hardwoods wouldn't work, but I've never seen them used. Just use your own imagination as you turn out your vases, bowls, lamps and plates. Experiment with different finishes and styles, and see which ones appeal to your friends and neighbors the most. When you determine which styles appeal to your market the most, concentrate on these styles.

Chapter 5

Make templates or jigs so that you can turn them out in large quantities. With a little practice, you'll be shocked at how fast you can turn out a vase that wholesales for $5.00, or can be sold at an art show for $10.00! The oddities seem to have the most sales appeal -- a knot that was hidden until you exposed it with your tools, a section of decayed wood that has the appearance of a medallion and becomes the focal point of a vase, and unusual grain. The plain vases and bowls sell well, but the oddities that you discover seem to bring the most money – and don't take any more time to produce. Most of these bowls and vases are sanded smooth, and sprayed with a flat sealer. They look great, and have a lot of sales appeal.

If you have a lathe, or have access to one, why not give this idea a try? Use your own imagination and see what happens. This would be a perfect job to start while you are still living in the city. You could set up your lathe in the garage or basement, get some dry soft wood and turn out a few pieces. Try to sell them at the local bazaars and flea markets, or better yet, try to wholesale them to dealers and gift shops. If you can establish a base to sell your work to, I doubt seriously that your buyers will care if you move to the country! In fact, your move to the country will probably enhance your image as an "artist"!

Example #7
Pottery and Profits

I have an acquaintance who is a potter. He and his wife produce beautiful bowls, canister sets, mugs and plates. His work is as good as you will see anywhere. In fact, we have five examples of his work in our house that we have purchased, or been given over the years. He lives a simpler life than I would find appealing, but he is able to earn a modest living with his art, and is his own man. He also has established a network of wholesale buyers for his art. In addition, he will take special orders -- make you a set of coffee mugs with your name on them, or a beautiful platter as a gift for someone with the name of their organization on the platter. I doubt that this takes any longer to produce than a normal piece would, but you can bet that you pay extra for the service, and are glad to get it.

He truly enjoys his work, and he is in his studio when the kids come home from school. He enjoys his life, and appears to be a happy man. Could you do something like this? Possibly not. But if you have the talent, and experience in an art form such as this, and are not afraid of hard work, then there is no reason for you not to give it a try. Just remember to keep the expenses as low as possible at the start, and keep in mind that you don't earn a dime until you sell something!

Example #8
Are You An Artist?

I know four people in my community who are painters. One of them has won several awards, and is able to make a decent living with her paintings. She exhibits them all over the State, and occasionally puts on a "one artist show". The other three people look at painting as a hobby, and once or twice a year, put their work on display for sale at bazaars and gift shows. Again, the secret here is to "paint what the people want" and then figure out a way to market your work.

If you enjoy painting, but are candid enough to admit that you don't have any "real" talent, then try to find yourself a gimmick. For instance, a few years ago, half the women in Texas were carrying hand painted lunch pails as purses. You could have done something like that. I have seen old shovels, hoes and tools painted with country scenes or animals. They must appeal to someone, and you could certainly do something like that. For a while, rocks glued together, and painted to look like creatures were popular (I personally could not understand their popularity, but why fight a trend?). You could do something like this – just remember the two "secrets" that I have given you about art. Better yet, come up with your own gimmick, and capitalize on it.

Example #9
Dance Your Way to The Country!

I have a friend that makes an excellent living teaching children to dance. She is a good dancer (studied in college, I believe), and enjoys teaching children. She teaches about 110 little kids (including two of mine) ballet, tap dancing and so forth, each week. She charges $15.00 per month per child, and I don't know a mother that would quit if she were to raise her prices! Every year she puts on a recital (everyone has to buy a ticket), and the auditorium is *packed* with adoring parents, grandparents, brothers and sisters. Could you do something like this? Certainly, if you have the talent. The secret is to get the town's leading mommies to enroll their little dancers. In small towns, the word gets out at school and at bridge luncheons, and before long, *everyone* wants their little one taking lessons!

Example #10
Teach, Teach, Teach

If you have any kind of musical talent, GIVE LESSONS! In most small communities, it is difficult to find someone qualified to give piano lessons, guitar lessons, voice lessons, and so forth. I have a good friend that teaches piano. She has her real estate license and worked hard at that profession, but I am certain that she has made more money in the year she has taught piano than she ever did trying to sell real estate. Follow the same rules for developing your clientele that was given under Example #8. Price your services by the month, and have a fair, but firm policy about paying for missed lessons.

I have listened to several children as they took their lessons, and believe me, you will earn your money! This area is one that is often overlooked, and let's face it, it would be difficult to earn a full-time living just teaching piano, but it could be a great part-time job, and could supplement your income while allowing you to do something else.

Example #11
Give Seminars

If you choose an area with a lot of retirees, give seminars on your specialty. If you can paint, sculpt, write, carve, arrange flowers, turn vases on a lathe, golf, make pottery or have any other special talent, GIVE LESSONS. Please don't think that I am limiting this opportunity to only the arts. If you have experience in auto repair, solar energy, hunting, fishing, backpacking, skiing, small engine repair, simple timesaving meals for working mothers, training hunting dogs -- if you have specialized knowledge about ANYTHING, someone will be willing to pay you for the information. I have seen real estate seminars where the first lesson was free. At this lesson, you were told how easy it is to become a millionaire, and how even you (yes, you) can become independently wealthy -- overnight! The rest of the course will cost $300, and yes we do take Mastercard!

If you have any specialized skill, there are people out there that will pay you good money to teach them that skill. Make sure that your fee covers not only your time, but the cost of any materials your class might use. You can charge per lesson, or for the entire course. My advice would be to have a set fee for a certain number of classes. That way, it won't cost you any money if someone is forced to miss a class one night.

Now I am going to give you a secret that will make you more money than the seminar will if you use it properly. Write your own "Personal Instruction Manual", and sell it at your seminar. It doesn't have to be long, or fancy (the fancier it is, the more you can charge for it, human nature being what it is!). You are going to have to write down your lesson plan, anyway, so why not spend a little more time on it, and turn it in to an instruction manual? After you have given a seminar or two, ask the class to write their comments on the class. Pick out two or three of the "most glowing ones" and get permission to use them. Then have these personal testimonials printed on the back of a fancy cover for your manual, and SELL YOUR PERSONAL INSTRUCTION MANUAL BY MAIL! Take out small classified ads in a publication that would logically be read by someone interested in your specialty, and see what happens. You will probably be surprised by the number of inquiries and orders that you receive!

Example #12
Start A "Penny Shopper"

There are many good ideas that can be transferred from one location to another. A good example of this would be "The Shopper". About eight years ago, an enterprising young couple saw the possibilities for a free newspaper. I'm certain that they got the idea for this publication while they were traveling around the country. These publications go by many names, "The Penny Shopper", "The Thrifty Shopper" and so forth. They are distributed free of charge, and are filled with free classified ads. The owners make money by selling advertising space to the major businesses in the area. Because these papers are free, the circulation can start off higher than would be possible if the paper were sold on a subscription basis. This high circulation is appealing to businessmen who are looking for the highest visibility for their advertising dollar. In our community, "The Shopper" is delivered free to every residence in town, and often contains pre-printed inserts from our local supermarkets. I have no idea what the supermarkets are charged for this insertion service, but I'm sure that it is profitable. Because of this high circulation and readership, the advertising rates are as high as those of a regular newspaper.

As time has progressed, "The Shopper" has become more and more like a weekly newspaper, with articles of local interest, TV schedules, comics, and because of the free classified ads, it maintains a very high readership. An interesting aside -- the county I live in has approximately 10,000 people, and we have six (6) newspapers! Since "The Shopper" came to town, only one of them continues to sell their newspapers from newsstands -- the rest of them are now free.

Could you do something like this? Certainly you could if you have any experience in the newspaper field. Come to think of it, the couple that started our "Shopper" didn't have any previous experience -- they just saw an opportunity, and capitalized on it! There is no reason why you can't do the same thing.

Example #13
Secretarial Service

"B" saw a need and filled it. She always wanted to have a business of her own, and she is an excellent typist, so she started her own secretarial and copying service. She rented an office that was centrally located and near our downtown area, yet had easy access. She started out with one typewriter and a copying machine, and types term papers (there is a small college in our community), letters, appraisal forms, resumes, and reports. She can bind booklets, and assists businessmen when their secretaries are on vacation or are ill. She works hard and makes a good living, and it was all her idea. It is a pressured-packed business, and I wouldn't enjoy it, but she makes a decent profit, and hires one or two ladies to help her when things get too busy. She now has enough business that she had one regular part-time lady, and she takes a couple of afternoons off each week to play bridge and bowl (and of course, when her son is playing in a ball game!).

Could you do something like this? Sure you could! If you are a good typist now, and can buy or lease a good typewriter and copying machine, you could get started today! You could start right in your home. Just print up notices on your copying machine giving your telephone number, rates and other pertinent data, and pass them out to anyone you think might have a need for your services. Once you are established, I think you'll be amazed at how much business you can generate.

If you are serious about a business of this nature, I have a couple of suggestions for you. First of all, the QWERTY keyboard (the keyboard found on 99% of all typewriters) was designed to *slow typists down*. When the mechanical typewriter was first invented, it was so slow that the operators were continually jamming the keys because they were so much faster than the machines they were using. The QWERTY keyboard was developed in an attempt to slow the operator down! It has been said that if you took all of the typewriter keys, put them in a sack, shook them up, and then randomly put them back on the keyboard, that *that configuration* would be faster than the keyboard you are using now! Years ago, a man by the name of August Dvorak invented a keyboard where all of the most-used consonants are under the home space keys of the right hand, and the most used vowels are under the home space keys of the left hand. This means that the majority of the words we normally type can be typed without taking your fingers off of the home space keys, and that approximately 90% of the words normally typed can be typed just using the home space keys, and the row of keys directly above the home space keys.

It should be obvious that this keyboard can greatly increase your production. However, there is a drawback. It will take from a month to six weeks to teach youself how to type on this new keyboard. If you are thinking about a typing business, however, it makes a great deal of sense to take the time to learn this new keyboard – simply because it will increase your speed by approximately 50%!! IBM makes a ball that works on a modified Dvorak keyboard, and several computers are designed to operate on the Dvorak system, which brings up my second suggestion.

If there is any way you can swing it financially, instead of buying or leasing a new typewriter, buy or lease a dedicated word processor with a fast, letter quality printer. The time savings (and time is your most valuable economic asset) that can be gained with a word processor are nothing short of phenomenal! On even the best typewriters, errors must be corrected manually. On a word processor, the error is corrected electronically on a monitor before the word is printed on the paper. One of my classic mistakes is to misspell a word "too short". For instance, with my lightening 60 word per minute speed, I frequently spell "mistake" as "mistak"! When you commit an error of that nature, you have two choices with a typewriter -- you can either run the "short" word together with the next word in the document, and hope that no one will notice the phrase "I made a mistakewhile typing", or you can put a smile on your face, quietly jerk the paper out of the typewriter, and start all over again. With a word processor, you can correct the error of omission by merely touching two keys. If you are typing long, boring lists, another classic mistake is to leave one of the lines in the middle out! If you have ever done this, you can remember how frustrated (mad!) you were. With a word processor, you can insert the omitted sentence, or paragraph, for that matter, with the touch of a couple of keys.

Just as I'll never understand how my wife and I were ever able to raise three children without a microwave, I don't understand how I was able to operate a business for years without a word processor! If you will try a word processor, I'll promise you that you will never be satisfied with a typewriter again!

The book you are reading now was prepared on a Zenith Data System with a Wordstar word processing program. I had three criteria that I was looking for in a computer/word processor. First, it had to be able to compute and print real estate appraisals, since that is my main line of work. Second, it had to be capable of writing business letters (and ultimately, the book you have in your hands) which meant I had to have a letter quality printer. Third, I wanted it to be able to process mailing lists. Because of the large amounts of data I must process in the Appraisal business, my computer had a 10.5 megabyte hard disk drive. If you can afford this added cost option, I highly recommend it. It will not only store an incredible amount of data, but the retrieval of that data is so much faster.

The Wordstar word processing program has an incredible number of options, and the capability to ease any typing chore for you. I was told by several "experts" that the Wordstar program was difficult to use. It is not. My wife and two of our children use it for everything from writing letters to compiling reports for school. If you can read, you can use the Wordstar program.

Just an aside, I started writing this book before I purchased my computer. I had a big-name electric typewriter with a correction feature. I gave up after one and one-half pages, simply because I had made so many errors in such a short time. The typed pages looked terrible because they had so many corrections, and I could see several places where I wanted to change the sentences around. I had already been looking at computers and word processing programs, and even at that early stage, it was obvious that trying to proceed on a typewriter was just a waste of effort! I have tried to convince "B" that her business efficiency could be greatly increased if she would buy a dedicated word processor, but they are expensive. I've told her, and I'll tell you, that if you ever use a computer/word processor, you will never be satisfied with a typewriter again!

If you are interested in learning more about personal computers and word processors, I heartily recommend

"The Personal Computer Book" and "The Word Processing Book", both written by Peter A. McWilliams. These books are available at any computer store, and in most book stores. Mr. McWilliams explains a difficult subject with humor and simplicity. Highly recommended.

Example #14
Use a Computer to Move to The Country!

In the previous example, I discussed how a home computer could be used in a typing business. Since I have owned my computer, I have come across several ideas that might be useful for small businesses in a rural environment. I have not seen anyone using these examples, but there is no reason that I can think of why they would not be successful.

In addition to the typing service covered above, you could create and mail out multiple letters for local businesses. For example, you could create a sales letter for a small businessman, and mail this letter to all of his good charge account customers. This letter could offer a special price on a specific item, simply because the recipient of the letter has been such a good customer in the past. With the "Mailmerge" function of your word processing program, you could type the same letter 50, 150, 1,000 times for him, with each envelope and letter personally typed with each individual customer's name on the letter! A personal letter, properly prepared, is a powerful selling tool.

You could buy an accounting program for your computer, and keep accounting records for small businessmen. Small businessmen are notoriously poor records keepers. You could provide a weekly service for them whereby you pick up their weekly receipts and expenses, and two days later provide them with a print out showing them how much they took in, and how much they paid out. At the end of each month, they would get an itemized profit and loss statement for the month. Most small businessmen don't know until the end of the year whether they have made any money or not, and by then it is usually too late to make any tax saving adjustments. If you could get ten or fifteen accounts like this, and charge them $50 a month for your service, you would have the basis for a profitable business. If you have any accounting or bookkeeping skill, this would be a natural for you.

You can purchase a program for your computer that enables you to prepare Income Tax Returns. When added to the service described above, you have the basis for a full time business.

If you have the "Mailmerge" function in your word processing program, you can maintain mailing lists for local churches, fraternal organizations, clubs. As any secretary will tell you, maintaining and purging mailing lists is a time consuming, disgusting job. With the "Mailmerge" function, you can type up the lists, and then purge them with the touch of a button. For large mailings, you can have every label printed alphabetically or if necessary, by zip code – all with the touch of a button! Because it takes so little time to manage a mailing list once you have it stored in your computer, you can keep your rates low. Your low rates can be your biggest selling point with the secretaries of these organizations, simply because the maintenance of a mailing list is so difficult to do manually.

If you have the talent for it, write programs for computers. It takes a special type of personality to write a computer program because it is so tedious. But if you have the patience to write a program, you could have the next million dollar seller computer game. You could also teach businessmen to use the computers that they already have! Most businessmen are like me -- they have a specific use for their computer when they buy it. They don't want to know how it works, or how many RAM or ROM it has, they just want to know how it will solve a particular problem for them. In spending over a year looking at computers, and talking to dozens of salesmen, I came to the conclusion that the entire industry is geared to selling "bells and whistles," and not to solving specific business problems. I would guess that the majority of computers purchased for businesses are used to handle inventories, accounts receivable, accounts payable and payrolls. If you can sit down with the businessman and show him how the same computer that he purchased for these functions can also keep track of his stock investments, his rare coin portfolio, how he can win at blackjack or poker, his inventory of rare wine and so on, he will PAY you for this service!

If you know how to REPAIR COMPUTERS, you have knowledge that can be sold. Any one who uses a computer in his daily business quickly becomes dependent on it. When it finally breaks down (as *all* mechanical things do on occasion), he'll pay almost anything to have it fixed quickly. That is the key word – quickly. In most small communities, the normal process is to mail it to the closest major city. Although the service is usually good, it takes anywhere from three days to three weeks to get it back. You can earn a good living, and be a great security blanket for your community if you have the skill to repair a broken computer.

If you have used any of these ideas to make a living in a small community, or have come up with an original idea that you think someone else could use, WRITE A BOOK ABOUT IT! Information about how to make a living with a computer is in great demand, and you can make a good living providing this information if you have it. Writing a book is hard work, even with a word processor, but the word processor takes a lot of the drudgery out of the task.

Example #15
Make A Living With A Guide Book

If you have picked a scenic or historic area to move to, why not write a guidebook for the area? Most of the research can be done in the local library, and you can get some of the "old timers" to fill you in on a lot of the interesting details. You can review restaurants, tourist attractions, shops of special interest, hotels, motels, and so forth. The secret to making money with a guidebook is to sell ads in your publication to the local businessmen. Keep the purchase price modest (if you could get a financial grant from your local Chamber of Commerce, you could even *give* the guidebook away). Write in a breezy, interesting style, and fill your guidebook with your personal insights. If you can afford the printing costs, use lots of pictures and maps. If you can sell the local businessmen on using discount coupons in your guidebook, do it. When you are selling them advertisement, you can get them to tell you what appeals to them most -- 10% off any purchase, two lunches for the price of one, a free gift. This is good, low cost advertising for them, and when you get ready to sell them an ad *next year*, they will remember how many of the coupons were returned to them.

I know a man that is writing a guidebook like the one I am describing. He is paid for the advertisements in the book *before* the guidebook is even published. This allows him to pay for his printing costs with the advertisers' money, and not have any of his own invested! As with most everything in life, the key to making money with a guidebook is how you market it. I would suggest making small racks that set easily on a counter, and hold a dozen of your guidebooks. Take these racks around to the local businessmen, and sell them the rack and the twelve guidebooks for half of the list price. (You should have priced your guidebook so that you are still making a good profit, even at 50% off the list price.) Be sure to include not only the people that have advertised with you, but the people who have refused. By doing this, they will get an idea of how well your guidebook has been received, and they will be natural customers for your *updated* guidebook *next year!* Be sure to check on these racks on a regular basis, and sell replacement guidebooks when the supply gets low.

    You could also work out a similar arrangement with your local Chamber of Commerce, but here is another idea. Have an attractive, one page advertisement printed up for your guidebook. Have the Chamber of Commerce include this advertisment in every information packet they send out. Your advertising will be going directly to people that are interested in the area, your sales volume will be increased, and you will be helping out your local Chamber of Commerce. The increased number of your guidebook sales will enable you to sell more advertising at higher rates *next year.* You can also take out ads selling your guidebook, and place them in the appropriate magazines. Each state, and a lot of tourist areas, have their own magazines. You will have to decide which ones appeal to potential buyers of your guidebook, and use small classified ads to market your guidebook. I would remind you again that the greatest guidebook in the world will not make you a dime *UNLESS YOU CAN SELL IT!* Use your imagination.

    One couple that I know started a "Phone Book & Visitors Guide". It is full of beautiful pictures, maps, historical information, and of course, advertisements. It contains telephone numbers for every telephone in all of the towns in the area, the college, and a human services section. It also contains the address and meeting times of every club in the area. It is given away free, and is updated *every year!* One final comment, use a large, easily readable type-style. Some of your customers will have bad eyesight, and will not purchase your guidebook if the type is small and difficult to read.

Could you do something like this? Sure you could! All it takes is a little imagination, and the desire to try "something different". You could even get started BEFORE you make your move by checking on printing prices, getting the history of the area, obtaining maps and taking pictures. If you do publish your guidebook, all of your trips to the area, and your expenses while you are there are deductible from your Federal Income Tax. Think about the advantages -- a tax deductible move to small town of your choice! Because the tax laws change so rapidly, be sure to check with your local accountant, and use his advice on keeping records and filing the deductions. Just a thought -- since a small rural community really only needs one *good* guidebook, keep what you are doing as quiet as possible until you are ready to sell your advertisments. You wouldn't want anyone to use your idea first, and take away your ability to make good money for years to come.

Chapter 5

Example #16
Why Not A Restaurant Guide?

If you choose a resort area, why not publish a yearly (or bi-yearly) RESTAURANT GUIDE? Most people who visit a tourist area love to eat out, and one of the first questions they ask is "where is a good place to eat?" Your guide would cover each. List the menus of each restaurant, along with their prices. If they have a "house specialty", you could describe it, along with interesting articles about the history of the restaurant, the owners, and so forth. Give the hours and days of operation, and whether reservations are required. Give your own personal view of the restaurant.

If you wish to be completely objective, you could rate each separately, but this eliminates the possibility of selling ads in your guide to the restaurants being rated. My suggestion would be to sell each restaurant a page for say $100.00, and then use their suggestions when filling out their "page". Then make certain that every hotel and motel in the area has a supply of your booklet. You could leave the bottom half of the front page blank and have the motel's name printed on the front. Your restaurant guide could then be sold to the motel or hotel (at a modest price) for them to either sell or give to their guests.

Everyone wins with a publication such as this -- the tourist gets the information he needs, the restaurants receive a tremendous advertising promotion, and the motels and hotels provide a much-needed service, and have their name in front of the customer at the same time. You, of course, can gain a very good income by producing a guide such as this.

Could you do something like this? You could if you enjoy

eating at restaurants, and have the salesmanship to sell the businesses involved on your publication! After you have produced one of these guides, the second will be easier – and it is something that you could do in a neighboring town or city as well. Think about it.

Example #17
Video Tape Rentals

I know two guys who started a video rental business. They rent both video recorders and movies, and have about 900 titles to choose from. They were getting rich for a while, because they had the only shop of its type in the area, but now there are three other places in town that rent movies, including the local supermarket! One of their competitors now has over 740 titles to choose from. Everyone seems to be doing alright, but these guys could have made a "pile" if they had sold out early! One nice feature of operating a business of this type in a small community is the lack of worry about theft. Except for the loss of a couple of video tapes, I could only find out about the theft of one video recorder. The thief was from out of town, and used a stolen wallet-full of identification and credit cards to steal a video recorder.

Check with your accountant, but I think that the tax write-offs in this business should be fantastic. The tapes should have a short depreciable life, and the video recorders should be "written off" in two to four years, giving you some great tax advantages. Just keep a wary eye out for the competition. I am of the opinion that this can be a great business if you are the only video rental in town, but when the supermarkets start renting tapes, it may be time to sell your business to some newcomer who wants to move to the country! College towns seem to work best for a business of this type because the students have an incredible amount of disposable income, and they are always looking for "something to do."

Example #18
A Used Bookstore With A Twist

I am a "bookophile". I love to read. Many times I have looked into the possibilities of purchasing a bookstore, so that my reading material could be acquired wholesale. The big problem that I keep running into is the possibility of a town with a small population base having enough readers to support businesses of this type. Most small towns have a business, such as a drug store or office supply store that have a section of hardback and paperback books. In areas with a lot of tourist traffic, many gift stores and curio stores also carry an assortment of books. I have come to the conclusion that a good USED BOOK STORE may be the answer.

In the small community where I live, I have watched two used book stores go into business, hang on for a while, and then die. I think I know the reason. You *must* have a good location for your store. Not only must your location have adequate parking, but it must have high visibility. Both of the used book stores that I mentioned above had locations with adequate parking but were located in an area that was "out of the way".

I have often felt that the person who could find a use for the *second story* of downtown business buildings in small communities could get rich. In every small community I have visited, the ground floors of these buildings were rented or owned by retail businesses of some type. The upstairs were invariably either rented to a young attorney or dentist, or were vacant. This vacant second story in the busiest part of your downtown area is where you want to locate your used book business. Be certain that the stairway to your location is well lighted and pleasant to the eye. The stairs should be carpeted, and vacuumed daily. You *must* eliminate the "cavern" effect that most downtown stairways present. A little soft music would help, and shadow boxes containing some of your most popular books along the walls of the stairway will not only give off a little more light, but will tend to break up the climb to the top. When your prospective customers arrive at the top of the stairs, they should be greeted with a well lighted lounge area, and not rows and rows of dusty books. Make the main lounge area as pleasant and attractive as possible. Have plenty of room for coats, and for storing packages that your customers may bring with them. Have one corner set aside with toys and books for small children.

Have your books displayed in some logical sequence -- it really doesn't matter whether it is by title, or subject or author, but know where your stock is! If you have a special interest in a subject like westerns, romance novels, economics or science fiction, *specialize* in that area. Try to make contacts with other used book stores in your state or surrounding area, so that when a customer asks you for a specific book, you can check other sources if you don't have it in stock. Strive to offer good service. Your customers will be glad to pay for this special service if you can provide it.

It seems to me that a used book store would be more successful in a town that has a small college, but this may not always be the case. On paperback books, the normal procedure seems to be to purchase them for 10% of their original printed cost, and sell them for half of their original printed cost. The stores that trade books generally trade two of the customer's books for one of the store's books of similar quality. This builds your inventory, but you must be careful not to acquire books that are torn, have the covers missing or look like they might be harboring some form of exotic fungus. Be careful about buying books that won't sell, such as old "Business Law 101" books (any old college text books!) or old almanacs.

Now here is an idea that will make your used book business prosper if you will just do it -- sell your used books BY MAIL! I have only seen one person that does this, but it must be successful because there are people who love to read all over the country, and many of them are too far away from a bookstore to make regular purchases. You must be able to print up a list of your inventory, and mail this list out to book lovers all over the country. This means that a small computer is going to be a necessity because you *must* be able to keep track of your inventory, and a computer will be the simplest way to do it. With a computer, you will also be able to keep track of your customers, prepare mailing lists and prepare mailing labels for your mailings. You can place small classified advertisements in any magazines you feel would be read by prospective customers, and mail the people who respond to your ads your inventory list, complete with your prices and mailing charges (be certain to charge your customers for the postage and handling). The U.S. Postal Service will help you, because it has a special low rate for shipping books! Take advantage of it.

Now be sure to tell your customers that you also will BUY books by mail. Tell them how to price their books, package them for mailing and send them to you. Explain that you will only purchase books in good condition, and what titles you prefer. You might even have your own address labels printed up, and include one of these labels, along with your instructions for purchasing books with every order you SELL! Mail them your check for the books the day you receive their books, and make sure that *they* pay the postage when they mail their books to you.

As your used book business grows, sooner or later, you are going to have three requests for "Love's Savage Whatever" and you are only going to have one copy in stock. There are several ways you can handle this dilemma. You can (A) return their money, or (B) try to find the books for them. I would suggest writing up a statement of policy and including it when you send out your inventory list. Just tell them that you only have so many thousand books in stock, and every so often, several people will want the same title. Tell them that it is your policy to mail the books on a "first come, first served" basis, with preference given to customers that pay by cash or cashier's check (never wait for a personal check to clear). Most people who buy books are honest, and you will gain more goodwill by shipping the order immediately than you will lose to bad checks. Explain that you will either find the book for them within thirty days, or you will refund their money. Contact other used book stores in your area, and try to purchase the books you need from them, at wholesale prices of course! You might make up a list of needed books, and mail it to these dealers once a week. If you pay these people promptly, you will be surprised how well they will cooperate with you.

Since time is such an important commodity, you might want to explain to your customers that their order must exceed $5.00 because of the time it takes to fill their order. You might even offer discounts for orders over $20.00. Use your own imagination and develop your own style, but the economics of the used book business indicate to me that you need more sales than you can generate locally to make a good living selling books. Let's say that the average paperback book has a list price of $3.95. That means that you will be paying 40 cents for it and selling it for approximately $2.00. This means that you are grossing approximately $1.60 per book. It makes a lot of sense to try to sell four or more books at a time, and to consider giving progressive discounts for volume purchases. Since your gross profit is pretty well set on each book, you must concentrate on selling more books! This idea obviously appeals to me, because I love books. The main drawback that I can see is the length of time that it would take to get your store stocked with inventory when you are getting started, the difficulty in finding books that your customers order, and the amount of time involved in running the business.

Could you do something like this? Sure you could! If you are married, and one of you has a job, this would be a natural for the other partner. After you have been in business for a year, make certain that you have the business set up so that you and your spouse can take some time off together, and enjoy the benefits that YOUR rural area offers!

Example #19
Could You Write A Travel Guidebook?

Love to travel? Why not make your small rural area your base, and when you return, write a TRAVEL GUIDE. Don't copy the existing guides, but be innovative and original. For instance, write a guide book specializing in meals under $5.00, or pick one city, and write a personalized guide book about it. Use your imagination, and try to come up with something different. I would suggest writing a travel guide for handicapped people. You could discuss the problems of the handicapped while they are traveling; hotels, motels and restaurants that cater to the handicapped, places that offer discounts to the handicapped, and so forth. If you are handicapped, or know someone who is, use personal experiences. Tell about handicapped people who are actually traveling and enjoying it.

Most travel guides are filled with facts, but they are *dull*! Try writing a guide with some humor. Use lots of pictures and maps. Try to interview local people, and find out what they think the average tourist misses, and why they think it is important. Write a guide book for a certain *segment* of the population. For instance, I have seen several guide books for the young single person. How about a guide book especially for people over 60, or one especially for widows? You could get the endorsement of your local A.A.R.P. chapter and even let them help you sell it!

How much money you make on a project such as this depends (have you heard this one before?) on how many you sell. So before you begin to write your travel guide, I suggest that you develop a plan for selling it. Again, use your imagination and try to come up with an unusual marketing approach. Researching a book of this type can be hard, difficult work, but one of the advantages to be gained is the ability to write off your travel expenses on your Federal Income Tax. After you have published your travel guide, all of your expenses related to updating it, or publishing a new guide are tax deductible! The only thing better than getting paid for traveling has to be letting the I.R.S. help to pay for the trip! Check with your accountant before claiming any deduction, but this is certainly an added incentive to write a travel guide.

Example #20
Mail Order

Almost everyone that has dreamed of moving to the country has thought of starting a small, home based MAIL ORDER BUSINESS. The mail order business has a certain romantic attraction. I can just put a small classified ad in my favorite magazine, and sell thousands of widgets from my kitchen table. I can make the widgets out of old beer cans, and the world will beat a path to my door. My advice to you is "Be Careful". There are a lot of thieves and scoundrels out there. Stay away from chain letter schemes, envelope addressing schemes, party plans, companies that want to "set you up" in the mail order business, or selling some sort of chemical preparations through the mail. Most of these "plans" are designed to make the *seller* of the plan a lot of money, and only rarely do the purchasers of these "plans" make any kind of a return. Peterson's rule on mail order is, "If it Sounds Too Good To Be True, It Probably Is!".

In researching this subject, I have found that most of the "plans" being sold are designed to appeal to someone who is having financial difficulty, or wants to move to the country. Most of these "scams" can be eliminated, simply by reading one or two good books on the subject of mail order. If you are really interested in mail order, I suggest that you read "How To Start and Operate a Mail-Order Business", by Julian L. Simon, or "How To Get Rich In Mail Order" by Melvin Powers. If you invest your money in *ANY* mail order business before you read at least these two books, I have some swamp land that I would be interested in talking to you about! The failure rate for people starting in the mail order business is astronomical

--something like 96 people out of 100 that try to sell something by mail fail. Most of these failures occur because of a basic lack of understanding of the mail order business. The mail order business is essentially an *advertising* business. To be successful, you must understand how to advertise your product in a way that brings in a large quantity of inquiries. It is not enough to have the world's greatest widget, you must be able to tell people about it in such a way that they think they can not live another day without it. The selling of merchandise through the mail is an art, and not many people have the ability to do it successfully.

Mail order is one area where it doesn't pay to be "original". Be a copycat. Study successful ads (any ad that is repeated for more than two months is probably making its owner money). Go to your local library, and check back issues of magazines. If the ad has been repeated year after year, you can be sure that it is successful. Don't literally copy these successful ads, but change them around to fit your product. Use your imagination and creativity to figure out why the ads were successful, and then adapt these successful characteristics to your advertising. These successful advertisers have spent a lot of time and money developing their ads, and you can get a first-rate education by studying them.

One of the very best ways for a small operator to make money in mail order is to sell information. Books and pamphlets have several advantages. They don't spoil or go out of date. They don't break in the mail. They can be mailed at "Book Rate", saving you many dollars in postage. They aren't returned because they "don't fit" (in fact, they are rarely returned at all!). If you have a special talent, or an unusual way of doing something, write a

Chapter 5

book about it. It doesn't have to be a long book, or expensive to produce. Most new copying machines are perfectly adequate for reproducing small books or pamphlets. Just write your book like you were talking to a friend, and then have someone proof read it for you. Have a few copies printed up, and put a small classified ad in a magazine that you think someone interested in your book would read. You must might be surprised at the number of inquiries you receive!

Example #21
Day Care Centers

If you are a parent with small children, why not consider opening a DAY CARE CENTER. Since you may be staying home with the children anyway, why not make a business out of it. In recent months, the news media have treated us to gruesome accounts of child pornographers that have used Day Care Centers as a front. Because of these reports, *every* parent that takes their child to a Day Care Center is apprehensive. Your home-type atmosphere should be geared to eliminating this fear. Insist on regular inspections by both your local police and social services agency. Plead with your customers to drop in unexpectedly to check on how their children are doing. Go out of your way to promote a feeling of security for the parents -- they will pay you handsomely for this feeling of confidence. If you are qualified, teach classes for preschoolers. Social researchers have determined that a child's IQ can actually be increased during this period of a child's life, and that the transition to public school can be eased by proper training in preschool. Provide excellent lunches for the children, and charge accordingly for your services. Don't be afraid of price competition with other Day Care Centers. Stress the advantages of *your* Day Care Center, and parents will willingly pay the difference for the feeling of confidence that you will be giving them.

In many states, Day Care Centers are highly regulated. Jump though all of their silly hoops, and then display your certificate proudly in a prominent place. Plead with the agency to inspect your Center regularly. In fact, call them for additional inspections, and ask them for letters of recommendation, or better yet, copies of their inspection reports. You may be in the child care business, but you are actually selling "peace of mind" to the parents of your children. Every month, write each parent a letter, telling them how their child is progressing, and the activities that you have planned for next month. Cover areas that the child is having problems with, and explain what you are doing to help with the problem. With each child, find an area that he excells in, and be lavish with your praise. If you have attractive handwriting, a personal note would be appropriate. If not, type the letters. Better yet, write the letters, keep track of billing, the child's attendance records and progress on a computer!

 Could you do something like this? You could if you enjoy children and aren't afraid of hard work. If you care for ten children and charge $60.00 per week, you can make a good living, and still be with your family. Check with other Day Care Centers in your area, and find out what their standard monthly charge is per week. Make certain that your charges are above it, and then stress the quality and security of your Center. You will have all of the business that you can handle!

Example #22
Clean In The Country

If you have picked a resort area, start a CLEANING SERVICE. One of the hardest things for a resort owner to find is a reliable source of maids, janitors, and handipersons. If you have any managerial talent, use it to develop your own "corps of cleaners". The person in charge of the resort will welcome you with open arms, because one of his most difficult duties is to find, train and keep competent personnel. Solve this problem for him, and make yourself a good living at the same time!

In observing cleaning contractors in my area, the biggest mistake I see them making is their blindness in trying to pay their employees the least amount possible. These jobs traditionally have been minimum wage positions, but to really succeed in this business, you need intelligent, hard working people on your payroll. The best way to achieve this is to pay your employees a little more than they could make working at a similar task, and offer them bonuses for increased production. The obvious bonus is more pay for more production, but if you are using college age people (a natural for this type of business) maybe a trip to Mexico or to some other exotic spot would be a better incentive. If you live in an area that has a definite "tourist season", this is an excellent way to make sure that no one leaves before the season is over.

I would suggest that you develop an "esprit de corps" for your organization. Provide snappy uniforms for them (you can rent them at first) and stress cleanliness while cleaning. Stress honesty while on the job, and then YOU be honest with them. If there is a local softball league, or skiing team or bowling league, sponsor your employees if they want to play. Not only will it be great advertising for your company, it will increase your employees' "esprit de corps". Let them pick their own name for the team, and buy 'em a round when they win -- or lose. In short, treat your employees the way YOU would want to be treated, and you will build yourself a successful business that will not only give you a good income, but will enable you to enjoy the area you have chosen. If you have organized your business properly, you should be able to take Thursdays off, and enjoy your family.

Could you do something like this? Certainly you could. Just use your own good judgment, and keep your eyes open for additional opportunities. Cleaning in a resort area is a continual hassle for resort owners, and if you can provide them with a service that will eliminate their management headaches for them, they will greet you with open arms, and pay you accordingly.

Example #23
If You're Not An Artist, You Can Still Paint.

Enjoy hard work and being outside? Consider being a HOUSE PAINTER. There is a lot of money to be made painting houses, but you *must* learn how to bid a job properly. You must be able to estimate the amount of time and material each job will take, and this only comes with practice. The preparation of the surface will take as long, if not longer, than the actual painting will, so price your work accordingly. Any good paint store has lots of information on preparing the surface for painting, what type of paint to use, and so forth. What they won't tell you are the little tricks that only an "old timer" knows. I must be truthful with you -- I hate to paint! In fact, on life's great scale of things, I put painting right up there (down there) with digging ditches with a shovel, mucking out sewers and kissing camels. When I did have to paint my own house, an "old timer" who just happened to be painting the house next door took pity on me (I wasn't smart enough to sit under a tree for 30 minutes and watch what he was doing!), and told me some of the rules of the game.

First, never try to paint from a ladder. After a couple of hours, your feet start to resemble claws from the constant pressure of the ladder rungs. Buy or make yourself a set of ladder jacks. This ingenuous contraption fits over the rungs of two side-by-side entension ladders, and lets you stand on a 2" x 12" board that fits in the ladder jacks. If my description doesn't give you the picture, ask at any good paint store, and they can show you what a ladder jack is. Another alternative would be to buy or rent scaffolding. Some scaffolds have locking wheels on them so you can move them easily.

A second trick that he showed me was "to move the ladders only once". When you get your ladders or scaffolding set up, do everything before you move them. Brush any dirt off, scrape any paint off that is peeling, prime the bare spots, and then paint the surface without moving your equipment. If you are using two or more colors, have a bucket of paint and a separate brush for each color, and paint with both colors before you come down from your perch. A small thing, but it cuts the amount of time needed to paint a house by about a third -- and time, as you know, is a valuable economic asset.

If you are serious about this idea, assemble a crew and supervise them. Painters traditionally aren't paid much, at least in my area, so some of the ideas given in the previous example may help you to keep a good crew together. After you have painted a few houses, you will be able to develop a "feel" for bidding the jobs, and bidding the job correctly is the key to making good money in this business.

Advertise. Have an attractive sign made, and put it in the front yard of the house you are painting. Stress "quality work at a reasonable price", and be sure to give your telephone number in large print. Once your crew is painting, talk to the neighbors, especially if their houses need painting. They will be able to see the quality of work you are providing, and you can offer them a "discount" because you won't have to move your equipment so far. Have some business cards, bid forms and invoices printed up. These items are inexpensive, and make your business look much more professional.

Don't use cheap paint! As a contractor, you will be able to purchase your paint wholesale (every paint store has about five price lists, so just keep haggling until you think you have the lowest price possible), so don't skimp on the quality. You don't want the paint washing off in the first rain storm. I have always used a brush, but some of the new "power painters" sound appealing. Check them out, and if they cut down on your time, use them. I would worry about having to spend time masking the areas you didn't want to paint, and how a breeze would affect the quality of your job.

Carry insurance. A fall from the top of a ladder could be very expensive if you had to pay for it out of your pocket--especially if the injury was of a permanent nature. When you are bidding a job, try to get half of your fee when you start, and the other half the day you finish. This will cut down on your paper work, and eliminate the tendency for your customers to insist "that you just paint this old lawn chair as well".

Finally, try to work out any differences of opinion that you might have with a customer. Bid your work so that there is enough money to "allow you to go the extra mile" if you have to. In small towns, your reputation is especially important to you. Most of the problems that arise can be eliminated by getting everything in writing *before* you start the job, and 99.5% of the people you work for will be honest. If you do run into someone who won't pay you, and you have tried everything you can think of to please them, file a mechanic's lien on their house. I knew an old man who got his house painted every six or seven years, and never paid for the job. When he died, the mechanic's liens had to be paid off, with interest, before the estate could be settled. A rare instance, to be sure, but stealing is stealing, and should not be tolerated.

Could you do something like this? If you enjoy being outside, and working with people, it is a natural for you. In most areas of the country, you won't be able to paint outside all year, so just plan accordingly.

Example #24
Be A Mortgage Broker

This is a specialized field, but if you have the training, be a MORTGAGE BROKER in your small town. Most small rural communities may have a bank, but only rarely will they have a savings and loan. You will become one of the most popular people in town if you can broker loans for houses, farms and businesses. You must have the proper training and contacts for this job, but if you have these qualifications, you will be able to make an excellent living, and at the same time, provide your community with a much needed service.

Example #25
Build A Mini-Warehouse

If the community you are moving to does not have a MINI-WAREHOUSE, why not consider building one? These buildings are usually built out of concrete blocks, and contain no plumbing or heating. Some of the units can be about the size of a large closet, while others can be the size of a small garage. No matter what the size, the units must have steel doors that are strong enough to deter break-ins. Because of the low maintenance and lack of utility bills, these units can rent from $10.00 to $40.00 per month, depending on their size and location. If you had 100 of these units, and you could rent them for an average of $20.00 per unit, and could maintain an 85% occupancy ratio, just one of these mini-warehouses could make you a good living!

I have a good friend who has built several of these units. His sons help him with the construction, and he is able to keep the costs of construction low. Because of the nature of these mini-warehouses, you don't have to build them on expensive land, or make them fancy in any way. If you have cash, you can build them without borrowing any money, and then build more units as the need arises.

Could you do something like this? Sure you could, especially if you have any skills in the construction field. If you don't have these skills, or don't have the inclination to build the units yourself, you can have a contractor build them for you. If you don't know what you are doing, a contractor will more than save you his fee. My experience has been that you NEVER, NEVER hire a contractor on a cost-plus basis. Make him give you a "turn-key" bid for the project, and get three or more bids for the project so you will know you are getting your mini-warehouses built for the lowest possible price.

Chapter 6

SUMMING IT ALL UP

There you have it -- twenty-five examples of how others have made a living in the country. It is my hope that one of these ideas is perfect for you, and that you have already started making plans to make your move. If one of these examples gave you an idea for a business that wasn't in this book, and you are already making plans to move to your country place, then I have succeeded. The entire purpose of this book is to give you the inspiration and determination to make your move to the country.

Now I want to have a word with those of you who have read this far, and have thought of all the reasons why you *can't* make your move to the country. You obviously have at least a small desire to live the country life, or you would have never picked up this book in the first place. All I can tell you is that those reasons (excuses) that you are giving yourself will start to disappear if you will only start to plan your move. Are you afraid of failing? Better men and women than you have failed, and have gone on to be successful because they understood that every failure contains the seed of a greater success. Do you worry about leaving members of your family in the city? Two people that I know personally have moved their parents/children to their country place, and now life is better for them all. Do you worry about your ability to make a living in the country? Take a trip, and look around the town that you have selected. do you see anyone visibly suffering from malnutrition? I know of no examples of city folks that have moved to the country actually starving to death! If you actually did make a move to a beautiful country spot, what is the worst thing that you could imagine happening to you? If that thing actually DID happen, so what? would you be any worse off than you are today? If you lost every material possession you have, would you be any different than you are now, or would you simply be the same person with fewer material possessions? Too many people tend to make idols out of their possessions, anyway. And God seems to make funny things happen when we start worshipping idols.

pro-cras-ti-nate vt. *to put off intentionally and usually habitually and for a reason held to be reprehensible (as laziness, indifference to responsibility);* vi: *to put off intentionally and usually habitually and reprehensibly the doing of something that should be done; delay attending to something until some later time; be slow or late in doing or attending to things.* Source: Webster's Third New International Dictionary.

Most of you are going to procrastinate about making your move to the country -- for all of the reasons I have given above, plus some that I haven't thought of. If you found yourself agreeing with the basic tenets of this book regarding economics, quality of life in the cities and what the future holds, then you are being foolish if you aren't starting NOW, TODAY, to at least plan for your ultimate move to the country. The longer you wait to MENTALLY make the hard decision to make the move, the more dif-

Chapter 6

ficult the process will be. You may have trouble envisioning a life different from the one you are living today, but believe me, it's out there. All you have to do is open yourself up to it.

I wish each of you good luck with your move to the country. If you have read this book and have made your move, please be kind enough to drop me a note and tell me about it. I can be reached by simply addressing the letter to Gunnison, Colorado 81230. I'd love to hear from you.

RECOMMENDED READING LIST

ECONOMICS IN ONE LESSON by Henry Hazlitt. This is simply one of the best books available for someone interested in learning about economics. It is easy to read and understand, and will whet your appetite for more information on the subject. Highly recommended.

HUMAN ACTION by Ludwig von Mises. A difficult book to read, but probably the best book on economics available.

COMMON SENSE ECONOMICS by John A. Pugsley. I am not in complete agreement with his investment advice, but his introductory chapters are excellent.

AMERICA'S GREAT DEPRESSION by Murray Rothbard. If you are tired of hearing that capitalism failed during the "great depression", read this book. If you want to know what *really* caused the depression, read this book.

GOVERNMENT BY EMERGENCY by Dr. Gary North. An updated version of his "How You Can Profit From the Coming Price Controls". It is an excellent book covering price controls and what to do about them, why the government is in a jam, and what it will probably try to do about it. I discovered Dr. North's books several years ago, and feel that he is the best contemporary writer of investment books in the field. He is a Christian, has a Ph.D. in economics, and writes so that the layman can understand very complicated subjects -- a combination you don't find every day! His books are highly recommended.

SUCCESSFUL INVESTING IN AN AGE OF ENVY by Dr. Gary North. Ditto.

AN INTRODUCTION TO CHRISTIAN ECONOMICS by Dr. Gary North. One of Dr. North's first books. I came upon this book while trying to figure out the relationship between economic laws, physical laws and spiritual laws. If you are a Christian or are just interested in why things happen the way they do, then this book is for you.

THE LAST TRAIN OUT by Dr. Gary North. More good information from Dr. North.

THE ROAD TO SERFDOM by F.A. Hayek. An excellent book on socialism, and why capitalism is superior.

THE COMING CURRENCY COLLAPSE by Jerome F. Smith. A good book on why we are in the mess we are in and what you can do to protect yourself from what is coming.

STRATEGIC INVESTING by Douglas Casey. Interesting.

PRODUCTIVE CHRISTIANS IN AN AGE OF GUILT-MANIPULATORS by David Chilton. A fascinating book on envy, guilt, poverty and what the Christian community should and should not be doing about it. I've had a total of three copies, and have loaned them out. It's the kind of book that you have trouble getting people to return promptly! Highly recommended.

THE BIBLE The first investment guide you should read. This book explains the game plan, the rules, and why some investments are bound to fail. You wouldn't play the "Futures" market without reading up on commodity trading, would you? Then why try to play the game of life without reading the Instruction Manual? Inflation is not new, nor is the growth of the State into every area of our lives. It has all happened before, just as it is happening now. Get your copy out and blow the dust off the cover. Start with inflation, Isaiah 1:21-23. Then read the Book of Proverbs for some good investment advice. The answer to most of your investment questions is here, if you will just read it. Highly recommended.

NEWSLETTERS

RURAL REVIEW -- ECONOMIC ADVICE FOR CHANGING LIFESTYLES. I publish this newsletter Monthly. Each issue contains one occupation or business that has been successful in a small country town, or in the country. I go into the profitability of the business, how much start-up capital is needed, what to watch out for, errors to avoid, plus all the facts and figures I can dig out. It will be a complete start-up manual for the business being described, and will allow you to know before you invest a dime what the chances for success are, how much time you will have to devote to the task, and secrets that will give you the edge for success. In addition, I'll give you helpful hints on how to make the transition to country life, mistakes to avoid when you arrive, and ways to help you and your family "fit in" when you arrive. You can pay more for a meal than you will for a year's subscription to this highly informative newsletter. Send me a check for $50.00, and I'll start your year's subscription. If after two issues, you don't think RURAL REVIEW is for you, just drop me a note, and I'll refund your $50.00 in full, no questions asked. Mail your check to 211 South Main Street, Gunnison, CO 81230. You'll be glad you did!

REMNANT REVIEW. Published 22 times a year by Dr. Gary North, $95.00. P. O. Box 8204, Ft. Worth, TX 76112. Send him five bucks, and he will send you the latest issue. There are a lot of newsletters available and I have read most of them, but Dr. North's is the one I keep coming back to. He discusses current events, hard money investments, and easy to understand economic analysis. The blurb at the bottom of the newsletter reads as follows: REMNANT REVIEW, edited by Gary North, Ph.D., is explicitly Christian and pro-free market in perspective. It is an attempt to apply biblical analysis. REMNANT REVIEW does not comment on the stock market. c 1984. Highly recommended.

DAILY NEWS DIGEST. Published weekly by Johnny Johnson. $147.00, P.O. Box 39027, Phoenix, AZ 85061. This publication covers financial "happenings", hard money investments, and is especailly good at digging out important information that the "networks" seem to overlook. It is especially useful if you are busy, and don't have a lot of time to read.

★ FREE FREE FREE ★

INSTITUTE FOR CHRISTIAN ECONOMICS, P. O. Box 8000, Tyler, Texas 75711. This group will send you a FREE six months' subscription to "Tentmakers" and "Christian Reconstruction" if you will just drop them a line. Both of these newsletters are published by Dr. Gary North, and they deal with everyday economic problems and choices. They always make for fascinating reading, and I look forward to receiving them. I'm betting that you will find them so fascinating that you will send them the $10 or $15 they charge for a subscription after the free six months period has expired.

THE GENEVA PAPERS, P. O. Box 8376, Tyler, Texas 75703. This group publishes several different newsletters (generally only two or four pages long) on an assortment of topics, ranging from book reviews, to commentaries on Calvin. I enjoy them, but you may not. Ask them to send you a couple of issues, and decide if their publications are worth your time.

FEDERAL RESERVE BOARD. This publication comes out weekly, and enables you to see what the government has done to our money supply during the past week. It is pretty heavy stuff, but the graphs are easy to read, and will properly scare you, especially if you have read any of the above mentioned books on economics! Just write to them at The Federal Reserve Bank of St. Louis, Post Office Box 442, St. Louis, Missouri 63166. Ask for a subscription to "U. S. Financial Data".

COUNTY EXTENSION AGENTS. Every county has one, even in the largest cities. Look in the telephone book for the address, and then go by. They have lots of interesting books and pamphlets on rural living. Some of you may have the desire to plant a garden, raise a few chickens and maybe a goat – I don't! If you have any ideas along these lines, your County Extension Agent is a good place to start. All of the information is free and there really is some good information available. Be kind to the lady in charge. She can really be a lot of help to you.

STROUT REALTY and UNITED FARM AGENCY. Both of these real estate companies publish interesting catalogues of their offerings. These catalogues make fascinating reading, and can give you a "general background" on the prices of real estate in the area you have chosen. The catalogues are free. Look in the yellow pages of your telephone book for the number of these agencies.

THE PUBLIC LIBRARY. A great source of knowledge. Spend an afternoon checking their "Business" section, and see if you can find any ideas for a job or business. Check the reference section for information on the area that you have chosen, then write to all of the agencies that you can find the names and addresses for. Get all of the information that you can before you leave. For years, librarians have gotten a bum rap. They have been portrayed as stern women with their hair done up in a bun with a pencil sticking out of it. My observation over the past twenty or so years has been that they are attractive, intelligent, helpful people who will go to great lengths to help you if you will just ask! May their tribe increase!